THE IMPORTANCE OF INERRANCY

How Scriptural Authority has Eroded in Modern Wesleyan Theology

Vic Reasoner

Fundamental Wesleyan Publishers
2120 Culverson Ave
Evansville, IN 47714-4811

ISBN 978-0-9761003-9-3

Library of Congress Control Number:
2013949012

Preface

Writing in 1966, Stephen W. Paine, the great Wesleyan scholar and president of Houghton College explained,

> The school child would rather do anything than to be observably different from his group. So would the college student. And this is a strong tendency also with the scholar. The certain knowledge that one stands apart from the great mass of scholarship in his own field of professional activity is like hydraulic pressure upon the one who stands apart. It almost certainly impels those in the tiny minority to seek bridges and relief valves and reconciliations. And should it later be realized that these are not real solutions, it is almost easier to let them go and to join the majority.[1]

A generation later many leading Wesleyan theologians have dismissed the doctrine of biblical inerrancy as Calvinistic or fundamentalist. We are told that it does not matter if the Bible contains scientific or historical mistakes so long as it testifies to the plan of salvation. It is asserted that the Bible does not claim inerrancy for itself, and since no one has seen the original manuscripts, this doctrine of the inerrancy of the original autograph manuscripts is not a practical issue.

---

[1]Paine, "Maintaining the Witness to Inerrancy," *Bulletin of the Evangelical Theological Society* 9:1 (Winter 1966) 25. Dr. Paine was also president of the National Association of Evangelicals from 1948-1950.

But ideas have consequences. If we embrace the prevailing view that Wesleyans are not concerned with such obscure issues as biblical inerrancy, the ultimate conclusion this leads to has tremendous implications. Inerrancy is a watershed issue. John Wesley declared, "Nay, will not the allowing there is any error in Scripture, shake the authority of the whole?"

Yet the full inerrancy of Scripture is under unrelenting attack. I do not propose that this booklet is the last word on the subject, but for many concerned pastors and leaders in the Wesleyan tradition it may be the first word they have read in defense of biblical inerrancy. Thank you for your prayerful reflection as you take the time to hear me out.

Vic Reasoner

TABLE of CONTENTS

THE IMPORTANCE OF INERRANCY

How Scriptural Authority has Eroded in Modern Wesleyan Theology

The Bible was fully inspired by God, given without error, and is our final authority for faith and practice. God's Word is forever settled in heaven (Psalm 119:89). As God is eternal, so is his Word. The Church has always found great comfort and found great strength in the surety of God's Word (2 Peter 1:19).

Inspiration means God superintended the human authors, using their individual personalities, so that they composed and recorded without error his revelation to man. The purpose of inspiration was to convey truth. God is the source of all truth; truth without error. Therefore, inspiration demands inerrancy.

Inerrancy means that the Bible, as originally given, was free from error and that the human authors accurately recorded what God said. If the Bible contains errors, its authority is limited.

If the work of the Holy Spirit was to transmit revelation to the human authors and to superintend their writings, then a Bible with historical and scientific errors reflects on the capability of the Holy Spirit. The Bible is our final ***authority*** because it is the Word of God.

The Bible cannot be compartmentalized. If Scripture is wrong about the nature of its inspiration, it may be wrong about the doctrine of salvation. To negate a part is to destroy the authority of the whole. William Burt Pope wrote, "The Bible is one organic whole. Truth is in every part; the whole truth, however, is only in the complete Bible."[2] In other words, the whole is the sum of the parts. The integrity of the parts is equal to the integrity of the whole.

The Bible Claims Inerrancy

In his survey of the position of the Wesleyan Church on the Holy Scriptures, Bob Black makes the claim that the Scriptures themselves do not specifically claim to be without error.[3] But while the specific term "inerrancy" is not found in the biblical text, the concept is implied as I will attempt to show.

According to Proverbs 30:5 *every* word of God is flawless. "Every word of God is flawless; he is a shield to those who take refuge in him."

Here *tsaraph* means refined, as in the refining of gold. God's word is completely reliable since it has been refined. It is devoid of foreign elements such as error. The emphasis is on the purity of God's Word, devoid of error. It is absolutely pure because it has been refined (*tsaraph* - Psalm 119:140). "Your promises have been thoroughly tested, and your servant loves them." John Wesley explained it is without the least mixture of falsehood.[4]

---

[2]Pope, *A Compendium of Christian Theology* (London: Wesleyan Conference Office, 1880), 1:184. Pope's theology is considered to be the classic statement of Wesleyan doctrine. This statement sounds very much like the Chicago Statement on Biblical Inerrancy that the Bible is inerrant "not only in the whole but in every part."

[3]Black, "The Wesleyan Church's Article of Religion on the Holy Scriptures: An Historical Study of a Theological Statement on a Biblical Issue with Pastoral Consequences," Wesleyan Theological Symposium (June 2009), 6. Dr. Black is a professor at Southern Wesleyan University,

[4]Wesley, *Explanatory Notes Upon the Old Testament* (1765; rpt. Salem, OH: Schmul, 1975), 3:1804.

The process of refining gold is also used to describe God's word in Psalm 18:30, "As for God, his way is perfect; the word of the Lord is flawless" and in Psalm 119:140, "Your promises have been thoroughly tested, and your servant loves them." In both references the word *tamim* is used to describe its perfection. *Tamim* is used of animals without blemish. It also describes "what is complete, entirely in accord with truth and fact."[5] Joseph Benson said the word of the Lord is free from deceit as gold refined by fire.[6]

"And the words of the Lord are flawless, like silver refined in a furnace of clay, purified seven times" (Psalm 12:6). Here "flawless" (*tahor*) is used of pure gold without alloy. The emphasis of this word is upon the state of the gold at the end of the process. It stands as a pure product.

These metaphors are borrowed from the refining process. The focus on the pure product is meant to convey the concept that all Scripture is without error. The statement that God's Word is like silver refined seven times probably expresses the concept of absolute purity or total freedom from imperfection.

In 2 Samuel 22:31 and Psalm 18:30, the way of God is perfect and the word of God is flawless. Here the word *tamim* is used of God's attributes. The word *tsaraph* is used of God's revelation. Because of the nature of Hebrew parallelism, the two descriptive words are being used as synonyms.

Two verses later, in both passages, David declared that God made his way perfect (*tamim*). Thus, God's way and God's word are both absolutely perfect. Joseph Benson said the word of the Lord is free from deceit as gold refined by

---

[5]Francis Brown, S. R. Driver, and Charles A. Briggs, *Hebrew and English Lexicon of the Old Testament* (Oxford: Claredon, 1907), 1071.

[6]Benson, *The Holy Bible, with Notes, All the Marginal Readings, Summaries, and the Date of Every Transaction*. 1811-1818. Rpt. (New York: Carlton & Phillips, 1856), 2:708. Joseph Benson was an early Methodist. Clarke called him "a sound scholar, a powerful and able preacher, and a profound theologian."

fire.[7] *Tsaraph* is used in Deuteronomy 32:4 to describe the works of God. "He is the Rock, his works are perfect, and all his ways are just." His works *and* his words are pure and free from any mixture of error.

A straight literal translation of the Masoretic text of Psalm 138:2 reads, "For you have exalted above all your name your word." In the culture of the Old Testament, people already understood that the "name" of God was exalted above all things. On the other hand, to say that God exalted his Word above his very name or equal to his name would be an amazing claim for Scripture. The fact that Scripture is held in such regard by God himself shows the nature of it.

The teaching of Jesus Christ in Matthew 5:18 also implies inerrancy. "I tell you the truth, until heaven and earth disappear, not the smallest letter, not the least stroke of a pen, will by any means disappear from the Law until everything is accomplished."

Jesus said the smallest letter or part of a letter would not have to be altered. Clarke concluded, "The *words* of God, which point out his designs, are as unchangeable as his *nature* itself."[8] Ralph Earle observed, "Jesus used very strong language here to assert the authority of God's Word."[9]

In John 10:35, Jesus declared that Scripture cannot be broken. It is impossible for the Scripture to be annulled or for

---

[7]Benson, *Notes*, 2:708.

[8]Clarke, *The Holy Bible, Containing the Old and New Testaments: The Text Carefully Printed from the Most Correct Copies of the Present Authorized Translations, Including the Marginal reading and Parallel Texts; with a Commentary and Critical Notes, Designed as a help to a Better Understanding of the Sacred Writings*. 1811-1825. Rpt. (Nashville: Abingdon, n. d.), 5:70. Clarke was the great Methodist commentator.

[9]Earle, *Word Meanings in the New Testament* (Kansas City: Beacon Hill, 1980), 1:20. Dr. Earle was the founding New Testament professor at Nazarene Theological Seminary from 1945-1977. He was president of the Evangelical Theological Society in 1962.

its authority to be defied or denied. As Wesley gave pastoral counsel, he wrote concerning Christian perfection that it will be experienced if sought, "for the Scripture cannot be broken."[10]

Jesus declared that the word of God is truth, and we are sanctified or made holy by that truth (John 17:17). "Sanctify them by the truth; your word is truth." The word *aletheia* refers to things as they are or that which conforms to reality. The reliability and consistency of the sanctified life are tied to the reliability of the Word of God, which is an extension of the very character of God.

The Scriptures are holy because they come from a holy God. The Scriptures are also true because they come from the God of truth. The Scripture is perfect, and its goal is to prepare or equip us completely and perfectly, according to 2 Timothy 3:15-17.

> You have known the holy Scriptures, which are able to make you wise for salvation through faith in Christ Jesus. All Scripture is God-breathed and is useful for teaching, rebuking, correcting and training in righteousness, so that the man of God may be thoroughly equipped for every good work.

Eta Linnemann wrote that if the Holy Scriptures contain error or falsehood, it can hardly be said that,

> "*All Scripture* is God-breathed and is useful for teaching, rebuking, correcting and training in righteousness." Error and falsehood could not serve such a purpose. How can we dare to allege that there are errors in God's Word in some area of natural science, or history, or some other discipline — we,

---

[10]Wesley, Letter to Penelope Maitland, 12 May 1763. See also Wesley, "On Riches," Sermon # 108, 2.9.

> whose scientific findings of yesterday and the day before are already outdated today? Woe to us if we possess such audacity! Should we not be thoroughly ashamed to say, "Here is an error in God's Word?" How do we intend to endure the flaming eyes of Jesus one day when our learned books which propagate such things are consumed like chaff?[11]

God-breathed implies inerrancy. If God breathed out the Scripture, then the Scripture, being the product of God, must also be true. However Michael Lodahl wrote me saying, "This passage focuses very specifically on the Bible's function to "make you wise for salvation through faith in Christ Jesus" (2 Tim. 3:15). That surely sounds like a soteriological function."[12] But Daniel Whedon, writing in 1875, defined the "salvation" as including deliverance from "Jewish, pagan, and Gnostic error, from sin, condemnation, and death."[13] Today we could also add from New Age, Islamic, and Mormon error. Thus, salvation is a broad term and even incorporates refuting erroneous philosophies.

The following verse, 2 Timothy 3:16, does not limit inspiration to a soteriological function. According to 1 Peter 1:10-12, the Old Testament prophets spoke of the salvation which was to come through Christ. Yet the scope of their message was not limited to the first advent of Christ. They also foretold the rise and fall of world empires.

All Scripture is God-breathed and profitable for,

---

[11]Linnemann, *Historical Criticism of the Bible: Methodology or Ideology? Reflections of a Bultmannian Turned Evangelical*, translated by Robert Yarbrough (Grand Rapids: Kregel, 1990), 147-148.

[12]Lodahl email to Vic Reasoner, 12 October 2010. Dr. Lodahl is a professor at Point Loma Nazarene University.

[13]Whedon, *Commentary on the New Testament* (1875; rpt. Salem, OH: Schmul, 1977), 4:456. Whedon edited the *Methodist Quarterly Review* from 1856-1884.

- *Teaching*. The Greek word *didaskalia* describes the body of Christian truth held by the Church. Yet doctrine cannot be restricted to salvific teaching. According to Hebrews 11:3, creation was also a matter of Christian faith. "By faith we understand that the universe was formed at God's command."

Thus no restriction can be placed on the subject matter. Scripture is profitable regardless of the subject it addresses. This does not mean that Scripture is the only source of truth in these fields, since there is also natural revelation, but anything taught as truth in any discipline must not contradict Scripture.

- *Reproof*. Divine truth exposes falsehood and sin, erroneous belief, and ungodly conduct. It reproves any teaching which contradicts the Word of God.

- *Correction*. This word means to restore to its original and proper condition. Again no restrictions are placed as to what the Bible may correct.

- *Instruction in Righteousness*. This would deal with ethics and morality, as well as faith and holy living.

Thus, these four clauses cannot be limited to salvation because the result is that the man of God is thoroughly equipped for *every* good work. "Every" cannot be limited to the spiritual realm alone. "Every good work" would not only include loving God, but it would include loving our neighbor as ourselves. Loving our neighbor as ourselves would extend into the ethical, moral, social, political, and educational arenas of life.

"Faith comes from hearing the message, and the message is heard through the word of Christ." If saving faith is based on the Word, as Romans 10:17 teaches, then to destroy confidence in God's Word is to undermine saving faith.

Too often, however, fundamentalism has contended for the perfection of the Word *and* the sinfulness of the believer. But why should we contend for Christian perfection and then claim there are mistakes in the Holy Word of God? Why affirm the possibility of perfection in the life of the believer while denying that it is possible for God's revelation to be perfect? The Word is active in our sanctification.

Again in Psalm 19 the law of the Lord is perfect. The word "perfect" is *tamim*, which means without blemish or defect. It is trustworthy because it is inerrant. It is pure or clean, and it is compared to gold which has been refined from impurities. This precious Word revives the soul, makes wise the simple, gives joy to the heart, and gives light to the eyes. The result is that my errors are discerned; my hidden faults are forgiven, and I am kept from presumptuous sins. A text without blemish (*tamim* - adjective) can produce a Christian without blame (*tamam* - verb).

We maintain that purity by living according to the Word. "How can a young man keep his way pure? By living according to your word" (Psalm 119:9).

Toward a Theology of Biblical Inerrancy

The doctrine of inspiration means that the Spirit so superintended the process of revelation that humanity was temporarily elevated beyond error. Logically, the original autographs had to be perfect and without error if they came from an infallible God and were inspired by the Holy Spirit. God cannot err. The Bible is his Word. Therefore, the Bible cannot err. Thus, inerrancy is a corollary of the doctrine of inspiration.

"Whatever the holy, unerring, and faithful Father speaks is — simply by virtue of having come from him — holy, unerring, and faithful."[14] Thus, the doctrine of biblical inerrancy is based on the integrity of God.

The testimony to God's truthfulness is consistent throughout Scripture. He knows all things as they are. He cannot be deceived. His Word can be relied upon. Our hope of eternal life is guaranteed by the promise of God "who never lies" (Titus 1:1-3; Heb 6:17-18). "Let God be true though every one were a liar" (Rom 3:4).

It has been argued that God's sovereignty is not compromised by an errant text. Essentially this was the position of Karl Barth. More recently Kenton Sparks argued, "God does not err when he accommodates the errant views of Scripture's human audiences."[15] But God *cannot* lie (Heb 6:18).[16] Thus, an unbiblical view of the inspiration of Scripture leads to an unbiblical view of God's nature.

Yet the Word of God came through humanity. According to 2 Peter 1:20-21 the prophets of old were carried along by the Spirit of God as wind in the sails moves a boat along the water.

> Above all, you must understand that no prophecy of Scripture came about by the prophet's own interpretation. For prophecy never had its origin in the will of man, but men spoke from God as they were carried along by the Holy Spirit.

They did not write under their own impulse, but were impelled by the Holy Spirit. Typically those who hold to a

---

[14]Michael S. Horton, "The Truthfulness of Scripture: Inerrancy," *Modern Reformation* 19:2 (2000) 26.

[15]Sparks, *God's Word in Human Words: An Evangelical Appropriation of Critical Biblical Scholarship* (Grand Rapids: Baker, 2008), 256; 258-259.

[16]Wesley makes the same argument in *A Compendium of Logic* [*Works*, 14:179]. God cannot deceive, therefore absolute faith is due to the testimony of God.

more liberal theology have emphasized the Scriptures as a human production, while those who are more conservative have contended that the Scriptures were divinely inspired and thus incapable of error. Thus, the "Bible wars" could be characterized as ships that pass in the night. Both sides have contended for half of an axial theme and each side needs the other for balance.

Mark D. Thompson wrote that the doctrine of inspiration is routinely misunderstood as the elimination of all human involvement, as though inspiration was mechanical dictation. But Thompson then argues that if inspiration is the dynamic process of God's gracious self-revelation to the biblical authors, then God was directly involved in the production of Scripture. And God acts in keeping with his character. That which is God-breathed must be inerrant.[17]

Just as the living Word, the *logos*, must be understood theologically within the tension of the hypostatic union, so the written Word must also be understood within the tension of the human and the divine. But at creation, sinfulness was not an essential component of humanity. Thus, Christ in his Incarnation was fully human and yet not sinful.

W. B. Pope wrote that there are two incompatible concepts regarding inspiration: the belief in an Inspiring Spirit responsible for all spiritual truth and the hypothesis that the human element is liable to all the common infirmities of human composition. Pope reminded those who used the Christological analogy to explain inspiration that,

> It ought not to be forgotten that the human nature of our Lord was sinless and incapable of sin. If its upholders allow that the human element in the Bible is unsusceptible of real error, however affected by

---

[17]Thompson, "Toward a Theological Account of Biblical Inerrancy," in *Do Historical Matters Matter to Faith?* James K. Hoffmeier and Dennis R. Magary, eds. (Wheaton, IL: Crossway, 2012), 95-96.

infirmity, their doctrine may be made safe, and if safe, it is deeply interesting and instructive.[18]

As the International Council on Biblical Inerrancy framers explained, "We affirm that as Christ is God and Man in one Person, so Scripture is, indivisibly, God's Word in human language. We deny that the humble, human form of Scripture entails errancy any more than the humanity of Christ, even in His humiliation, entails sin."[19]

In the beginning God breathed into mankind his breath (Gen 2:7). In anticipation of Pentecost, Jesus breathed on his disciples (John 20:22). And Scripture is also God-breathed (2 Tim 3:16).

The same Spirit who overshadowed the virgin Mary so that the living Word was conceived without Adam's sin also overshadowed the human authors so that their word became the written Word of God without error. Why should that be hard for us to accept since we believe that the indwelling Spirit can also keep us from sin? Since Wesleyan theology has given a greater emphasis to the work and ministry of the Holy Spirit, can we not say that the perfecting grace of the Holy Spirit temporarily enabled the human authors and superintended the canon of Scripture so that we have the infallible Word of God? To deny that the Holy Spirit had the freedom to insure the accurate transmission of divine revelation through human authors does not seem very Wesleyan. The same Holy Spirit now uses that Word of God to perfect the Church of God.

---

[18]Pope, *Compendium*, 1:184-185.

[19]Norman L. Geisler and William C. Roach, *Defending Inerrancy* (Grand Rapids: Baker, 2011), 317-318.

Where Are the Original Manuscripts?

Historically, the canonical books were regarded by the early Church as inerrant.[20] Pseudepigriphal writings were never regarded as divinely inspired because they were in error regarding the true human authorship. It did not matter if the text contained truth. It was inconceivable that the Word of God would even contain incidental error.

God providentially has also preserved his Word across the centuries. We now possess over 5,700 New Testament manuscripts and some 10,000 Old Testament manuscripts and fragments. Yet these copies are not necessarily inerrant copies. The objection is raised that if the doctrine of inerrancy extends only to the original autographs and they apparently no longer exist, then we are contending for the inerrancy of a text we have never seen.

According to Dennis Bratcher this appeal to the original autographs as inerrant is unhelpful. He objects that this concept assumes a single person wrote individual books instead of the community of faith producing them over a period of time as God worked within the community. He then asserts that the Gospels were written from earlier sources.[21]

But here Bratcher is referring to the Quelle or Q source, which no one has ever seen. Source critics have suggested that the synoptic Gospels were drawn from this prior source. Yet it is not a logical necessity to hold to this theory. Matthew, Mark, and Luke could have been given by direct revelation and not through a theoretical sequence such as the two-source view

---

[20]John D. Hannah, "The Doctrine of Scripture in the Early Church," in *Inerrancy and the Church*, John D. Hannah, ed. (Chicago: Moody, 1984), 3-35.

[21]Bratcher, "Thinking about the Bible Theologically: Inerrancy, Inspiration, and Revelation," in *The Bible Tells Me So*, Richard P. Thompson and Thomas Jay Oord, eds. (Nampa, ID: SacraSage, 2011), 62-63. Dr. Bratcher is a professor at Point Loma Nazarene University.

which postulates that Mark was written first, then Matthew and Luke were dependent on Mark and Q. The four-source theory also postulates two additional sources which no one has ever seen — an M document and an L document.

But Bratcher dismisses the inerrancy of the original autographs because he has never seen them, yet affirms the existence of the Q source of the Gospels although he has never seen it. Thus, both positions are attempting to formulate their theology on the basis of their presuppositions. Why is that legitimate for source critics, but not for those who affirm the inerrancy of Scripture?

However, just because we have not seen the original manuscripts does not mean that they have never existed. According to Tertullian the original autographs of the apostles may have existed as late as the second century.[22] Through the science of comparative analysis, textual critics have reconstructed a faithful replication of the original manuscripts.

The Bible we have comports with the original autographs, so we do have the Word of God insofar as it has been accurately copied. Any textual discrepancies are inconsequential. The only significant variations amount to 1/1000 of the text or less than ½ of one page of the Greek New Testament.

Why did God not see fit to preserve the original autographs to this day? Perhaps they would have become objects of idolatry. But this is a question that only God himself can answer. It is like the question of the grieving parents who ask, why did God allow my child to die? God does not always disclose his ways to us. Admittedly, God *could* have assigned an angel to superintend the preservation of the original autographs, but error could have been interjected by copyists.

---

[22]Tertullian, "The Prescription Against Heretics," ch. 36 in *The Ante-Nicene Fathers*, Alexander Roberts and James Donaldson, eds. (1885; rpt. Grand Rapids: Eerdmans, 1978), 3:260. This evidence is evaluated by Daniel B. Wallace, "Did the Original New Testament Manuscripts still exist in the Second Century?" <http://bible.org/article/did-original-new-testament-manuscripts-still-exist-second-century>

Angels *could* have been assigned to oversee each copy that was made, but error could have been interjected in translation.

Again, if angels preserved the truth in preservation, the making of copies, and in translation, why were not angels assigned to every human messenger to prevent the preacher from misinterpreting the text?

However, with regard to the preservation of the original autographs, I think the answer must be found in the balance of divine sovereignty and human responsibility. God revealed through divine inspiration, but that revelation can no longer be isolated to one manuscript. It must be reconstructed through textual criticism. The original text exists today in the copies and the apparatus and can be reconstructed by comparative analysis to over 99% accuracy. Thus, the concern about whether the text we now have is accurate has been greatly exaggerated. W. B. Pope articulated the classic Wesleyan position,

> It has pleased God to commit His eternal counsels to human language, and to human language under all the penalty of Babel. From age to age he has raised up men to utter His words to their fellow men in their own fleeting speech, and to deposit those words in documents which were not visibly shielded from the vicissitudes of all human things. He did not create for revelation a dialect that should never change, or write it upon tables that might defy the hand of man or the breath of time to destroy them. The ancient tongues of the earliest revelation are now dead languages. The original autographs are lost; nor is there a single sentence extant written by inspired fingers. God's book, like the books of men, has been transcribed and continually reproduced; it has been translated, and must be translated into all the languages of the earth, more or less suffering, *for*

a season if needs be, in the process. Christendom does not remember, nor ever can now retrieve, any one central authoritative copy. Such an archetypal Bible might indeed have been preserved in the ark of the church, even as the law was long preserved in the ark of the sanctuary, from the waters of oblivion. It had been a light thing for Omnipotence to do this. But God has ordered it otherwise: and in ordering it otherwise, He has protected His people from the danger of enshrining and worshipping a book, whilst He has given their faith in perpetuity one of its sublimest exercises.

The church's faith in the permanent integrity of the written word has every presumption in its favour, is sustained by the express assurance of Scripture itself, and is justified by the results of Christian learning.

If God has condescended to inspire holy men to announce and write His will in a book, can we suppose that He would permit their writings to be abandoned to all the chances of time and all the caprices of men? that He would suffer His holy word to see corruption? The very thought is like the first shaking of the foundations. And what man's instinct suggests, the Bible every where, and with express emphasis, declares, that as the word of God its every jot and tittle is under a mysterious but most certain defense: with no less assurance than it appeals to inspiration for its origin does it appeal to a special omnipotent Providence for its preservation. Skeptical criticism cannot deny that the Bible contains substantially the same documents as were received by the faith of the church before and after Christ. And reverent criticism glories in her function, as the handmaid of the Holy Ghost, gradually and surely to restore to the sight of man what to the eye of God has always existed amongst the diversified copies, —the true and faithful sayings which first sprang from inspiration. Concerning some of the jots and tittles of the word we may for a time hang in doubt; but our faith is assured that there is no uncertainty in the Holy Spirit. The foundation of God's word also standeth sure, having this seal. *The Lord knoweth the words that are His*. And we also may yet have absolute certainty. Before the holy volume is rolled up again for ever, it will shine forth in all its faultless glory.[23]

Does It Matter If the Bible Contains Historical Mistakes?

The message of Scripture is set in "time and space." Mark Noll observed that the Christian faith has an irreducible historical character.[24] Would it matter if we held that the Jewish exodus from Egypt symbolizes salvation, but the actual historical account of the exodus is unimportant? The Mormon scriptures also depict a plan of salvation, but evangelicals reject these books because they contain anachronisms and historical inaccuracies.[25] Shall we simply focus on the salvation message in the books of Mormonism and ignore these inaccuracies as unimportant details?

In response to the claim by Soame Jenyns that the writers of Scripture were sometimes left to themselves, and consequently made some mistakes, Wesley declared, "Nay, if there

---

[23]Pope, *The Abiding Word* (London: Wesleyan Conference Office, 1855), 7-8.

[24]Noll, *Turning Points: Decisive Moments in the History of Christianity* 2nd ed. (Grand Rapids: Baker, 2000), 15

[25]Gleason L. Archer, Jr, *A Survey of Old Testament Introduction* (Chicago: Moody, 1974), 501-504.

be any mistakes in the Bible there may as well be a thousand. If there be one falsehood in that book, it did not come from the God of truth."[26]

That is why early Methodism held to full inerrancy, although in those days it was sufficient to speak of the infallibility of Scripture. John Wesley wrote concerning the Holy Scriptures,

> This is that *word of God which remaineth for ever*: of which, though *heaven and earth pass away, one jot or tittle shall not pass away*. The Scripture therefore of the *Old and New Testament* is a most solid and precious system of Divine truth. Every part thereof is worthy of God; and all together are one entire body, wherein is no defect, no excess.[27]

In the introduction to his notes on the book of Proverbs Wesley said,

> And these Proverbs of Solomon are not merely a collection of the wise sayings which had been formerly delivered, but were the dictates of the Spirit of God in Solomon; so that it is God by Solomon that here speaks to us.[28]

In his comments on 1 Corinthians 2:13, Wesley wrote that the words of Scripture are words taught by the Holy Spirit. "How high a regard ought we then to retain for them!"[29]

---

[26]Wesley, *Journal*, 24 July 1776.

[27]Wesley, Preface to *Explanatory Notes upon the New Testament* (1754; rpt. Salem, OH: Schmul, 1976), ¶ 10, p. 5.

[28]Wesley, *Notes*, 3:1830.

[29]Wesley, *Notes*, 412.

Wesley did acknowledge that difficulties exist in reconciling the genealogies of Matthew and Luke. Wesley argued that both writers worked with the material to which they had access. "Nor was it needful they should correct the mistakes, if there were any."[30] But it should be noted that Wesley did not affirm mistakes in the genealogy.

Wesley's position is compatible with the Chicago Statement of Biblical Inerrancy, Article XIII, which denies that inerrancy is negated "by Biblical phenomena such as a lack of modern technical precision, irregularities of grammar or spelling, observational descriptions of nature, the reporting of falsehoods, the use of hyperbole and round numbers, the topical arrangement of material, variant selections of material in parallel accounts, or the use of free citations."[31]

Wesley declared, "My ground is the Bible. Yea, I am a Bible-bigot."[32] He was a "man of one book."[33] If you claim to have a better way, Wesley demanded, "Show me it is so by plain proof of Scripture."[34] His sermons constantly appealed to the Scriptures — the law and the testimony. He explained, "In every point I appeal 'to the law and the testimony' and value no authority but this."[35] A favorite expression for Wesley was

---

[30]Wesley, *Notes*, 10.

[31]Daryl McCarthy, "Wesleyan Founders and Scripture," *The Arminian Magazine* 27:1 (Spring 2009) 10-11.

[32]Wesley, *Journal*, 5 June 1766.

[33]Wesley, *Preface* to Sermons, ¶ 5; "On God's Vineyard," Sermon # 107, 1.1; *The Bicentennial Edition of the Works of John Wesley* [*BE*] (Nashville: Abingdon, 2013), 13:145; *Letter* to John Newton, 14 May 1765.

[34]Wesley, *Preface* to Sermons, ¶ 9.

[35]*The Works of John Wesley*, Thomas Jackson, ed. 3rd ed. (1872; rpt. Grand Rapids: Baker, 1979), 9:467.

to describe the Scriptures as "the oracles of God."[36] He also called Scripture "words taught by the Holy Spirit," and "the words of God and not of man."[37]

He described the Bible as the one, "the only standard of truth."[38] Wesley preached, "'All Scripture is given by inspiration of God' (consequently, all Scripture is infallibly true)."[39]

In 1762 Wesley confronted William Warburton, the Bishop of Gloucester. Warburton had written that the Holy Spirit had "so directed the writers, that no considerable error should fall from them." But Wesley replied, "Nay, will not the allowing there is *any error* in Scripture, shake the authority of the whole?"[40]

Scott Jones explained that Wesley's view of inerrancy functioned as a "negative guarantee that the Scriptures are without error . . . and as a positive guarantee that the Scripture is unquestionably true, perfect, and consistent."[41]

Richard Watson declared,

> But their plenary inspiration consisted in this, that they were kept from all lapses of memory, or inadequate conceptions, even on these subjects; and on all others the degree of communication and influence, both as to doctrines, facts, and the terms in which

---

[36]Wesley, "The Almost Christian," Sermon #2, 2.3; "The Means of Grace," Sermon #16, 3.9; "The Nature of Enthusiasm, Sermon #37,¶ 22; "Christian Perfection," Sermon #40, ¶ 2; *Journal*, 28 January 1741; *Notes*, 397; *BE Works*, 13:141.

[37]Wesley, *Notes*, 412; "Christian Perfection," Sermon #40, ¶ 3. In context Wesley was defending the use of the word "perfect."

[38]Wesley, *BE Works*, 13:137.

[39]Wesley, "The Means of Grace," Sermon #16, 3.8.

[40]Wesley, *BE Works*, 11:504.

[41]Scott Jones, *John Wesley's Conception and Use of Scripture* (Nashville: Kingswood, 1995), 25.

> they were to be recorded for the edification of the Church, was proportioned to the necessity of the case, but so that *the whole* was authenticated or dictated by the Holy Spirit, with so full an influence, that it became truth without mixture of error, expressed in such terms as he himself ruled or suggested.[42]

Adam Clarke concluded, "Men may err, but the Scriptures cannot; for it is the *Word of God* himself, who can neither mistake, deceive, nor be deceived."[43]

As early as 1862 Samuel Wakefield anticipated the weakness of limited inerrancy.

> Some who advocate the doctrine of Divine inspiration limit it to the prophetical parts of Scripture; while others extend it to the *doctrinal* parts also, but not to the historical. There are many who maintain that the inspiration of the sacred writers was only occasional; that they were not always under that immediate and plenary [full] influence of the Holy Spirit which renders their writings the unerring word of God; and that consequently, as they were sometimes left to themselves, they then thought and reasoned like ordinary men. According to this notion, an intermixture of human infirmity and error is by no means excluded from the Sacred Scriptures. But if it is once granted that they are in the least

---

[42]Watson, *Conversations for the Young: Designed to Promote the Profitable Reading of the Holy Scriptures* (London: John Mason, 1830), 14-15. See also Watson, *Theological Institutes* (1823-1829; rpt. New York: Hunt & Eaton, 1889), 1:248. Watson was the first Methodist systematic theologian.

[43]*The Miscellaneous Works of Adam Clarke*, James Everett, ed. (London: T. Tegg, 1836-1837), 12:132, see also Clarke, *Commentary*, 5:11.

> degree alloyed with error, an opening is made for every imaginable corruption. And to admit that the sacred writers were only occasionally inspired, would involve us in the greatest perplexity; because, not knowing when they were or were not inspired, we could not determine what parts of their writings should be regarded as the infallible word of God. To tell us, therefore, that they were inspired only on certain occasions, while we have no means of ascertaining what those occasions were, is the same as to say that they were not inspired at all.[44]

Writing on the inerrancy of the sacred Scriptures in 1894, D. G. W. Ellis declared,

> Those who feel called upon to defend the inerrancy of the Scriptures do not hesitate to allow numberless errors and inaccuracies in all the translations of the sacred volume now extant. . . . The claim of inerrancy belongs only to the *original* writings of inspired men who spake and wrote as they were moved by the Holy Ghost. . . . Those who deny the inerrancy of the original writings of these sacred books admitted into the canon of scripture must do so, I think, because they are not willing to believe in the supernatural.[45]

While the genre of the book of Proverbs is not narrative, much of the Bible tells a story. The irony is that "narrative preaching" is popular, but for some preachers the biblical narrative itself is not trustworthy? Roger Olson wrote,

---

[44]Wakefield, *A Complete System of Christian Theology* (1862; rpt. Salem, OH: Schmul, 1985), 77-78.

[45]Ellis,"Inerrancy of the Sacred Scriptures," *The Quarterly Review of the Methodist Episcopal Church, South* 16:2 (July 1894) 234.

> It took quite a while for me to discern that the pastor of the church we were attending was theologically liberal. That was because he preached stirring, biblically based sermons, and delivered meticulous Bible studies. I gradually began to detect, however, that he did not necessarily believe that the "truth" of the biblical stories he loved to explore and explain had any connection with objective time-and-space history. During a private conversation one Sunday morning, he revealed his true hermeneutical impulses to me: "You know," he stated, "I don't really think it matters whether any of these beautiful stories of what the Bible describes actually happened. All that really matters is their transforming power in people's lives." My family and I left that church within weeks.[46]

According to John 14:11, we should believe Christ on the basis of what he has done. How can we know what he has done if the historical record is unreliable?

The many convincing proofs, which are appealed to in Acts 1:3, essentially are historical. According to 1 Corinthians 15:14, if the resurrection did not actually happen in time and space, then our faith is in vain.

Does It Matter If the Bible Contains Scientific Mistakes?

In Romans 1, Paul appeals to creation as proof that there is a God and that the pagans should seek him. This passage connects salvation and science. While the primary teaching of the Bible is God's redemptive program through Jesus Christ in providing this salvation, God entered our world to deal with us in our history and geography. The record of God's salvation,

---

[46]Olson, "Back to the Bible [Almost],"*Christianity Today* 40:6 (20 May 1996) 34.

thus, touches other areas of knowledge as well as spiritual truth. This does not mean the writers knew more about history and science than people do today, but it does mean that God preserved them from misleading us in any statement.[47]

In 1894 D. G. W. Ellis submitted an article to *The Quarterly Review of the Methodist Episcopal Church, South* in which he advised ministers who reject the infallibility of God's Word to promptly resign. Ellis went on to chastize T. H. Huxley, who called himself "Darwin's Bulldog," for rejecting Genesis 1. Ellis declared, "The account of the creation given in the first chapter of Genesis requires less credulity on the part of those that believe it than is necessary to the acceptance of the speculations of scientists."[48]

It is significant that this article comes over twenty-five years before the term "fundamentalist" was coined. Ellis was defending historic Methodist doctrine, connecting plenary inspiration, infallibility, and inerrancy, while rejecting evolutionary theory in the realm of science and biblical criticism.

However, in *Square Peg: Why Wesleyans Aren't Fundamentalists*, it appeared that the chief reason why Wesleyans cannot be fundamentalists is that fundamentalism rejects evolutionary theory. While the modern intelligent design movement is in the process of burying the remains of evolutionary theory, these philosophes are running to jump aboard the train just as it is grinding to a halt. They exemplify what Paul described in Romans 1:22.[49]

While God certainly knew the processes of creation, they ask what sense would it make to explain it to people who had no scientific frame of reference in which to understand it? The answer is divine revelation. God is revealing truth to us that

---

[47]Robert L. Saucy, *Scripture* (Nashville: Word, 2001), 158.

[48]Ellis,"Inerrancy of the Sacred Scriptures," *The Quarterly Review of the Methodist Episcopal Church, South* 16:2 (July 1894) 236; 238.

[49]*Square Peg*, Al Truesdale, ed. (Kansas City: Beacon Hill, 2012).

we would not otherwise know. While he accommodated his revelation to the limitations of our vocabulary, and while it is quite possible that those human messengers who were used in the process of inspiration may not have fully understood the message, the truth is that what God spoke is the most accurate historical and scientific account of creation that we will ever have. The purpose of accommodation is clarity, and the limit of accommodation is deceit.

The claim that the Old Testament picture of the universe is prescientific and therefore must be reinterpreted in the light of modern scientific theory makes biblical revelation inferior to modern scientific theory. Israel did not borrow this worldview from their surrounding neighbors. The distorted record of their surrounding neighbors is testimony to a universal revelation of God through nature and through inspiration that was eventually suppressed.

It is disappointing to see the contributors of this book trot out the old, tired, claim that the Hebrew word *yom* can mean an indeterminate period of time. *Yom* the word for "day" can be used figuratively, but whenever it is qualified by a number, it always means a twenty-four hour period. *Yom* occurs 1704 times in the Old Testament, and most of its uses refer to the normal cycle of daily earth time, unless the context compels otherwise.

In the Pentateuch, in 119 cases where *yom* is used with a numerical adjective, it always means a literal day. This is also true of 357 instances outside the Pentateuch. All 608 uses of the plural "days" are literal.

It is true that the sun was not created until the fourth day, but apparently the first three days were of the same length in anticipation of the first solar day. The phrase "evening and morning" occurs over a hundred times in the Old Testament, always with reference to a 24-hour day. The fourth commandment is based on the presupposition that the six days are all 24 hour periods (see Exodus 20:11).The point is that we have a

Sabbath, one day in seven, which is based on his creative week.

If H. Orton Wiley claimed that the first three chapters of Genesis were poetic, then he was wrong. Milton S. Terry wrote, "Any satisfactory interpretation of Genesis must be preceded by a determination of the class of literature to which it belongs." And then he said, "every thorough Hebrew scholar knows that in all the Old Testament there is not a more simple, straight forward prose narrative than this first chapter of Genesis."[50]

While the theory of evolution has never been proven and while most Americans reject it, apparently we who are fundamental Wesleyans are an embarrassment to the "Wesleyan" philosophes. In their recent book *The Anointed* (2011) Randall J. Stephens and Karl W. Giberson, both professors at Eastern Nazarene University, joined forces with atheists to form the Darwin lobby. In so doing, they seek favor with mainstream academia and have betrayed their holiness heritage of separation from the world.[51]

I am reminded of the words of Thomas Oden, "The most maligned and mutilated and demeaned are believers who bear the unfair epithet of 'fundamentalist,' like the Jews who wore the Star of David on their clothes in Nazi Germany."[52]

---

[50]Terry, *Biblical Hermeneutics* 2nd ed. (1885; rpt. Grand Rapids: Zondervan, 1974), 548. Terry was a transitional American Methodist theologian. I am aware of the shifts in his theology. I document them in Reasoner, *Hope of the Gospel* (Evansville, IN: Fundamental Wesleyan, 1999), 280-287. I am aware that he omitted the entire chapter from which this quote was taken in the third edition of *Biblical Hermeneutics* (1890). I can only reply that he was right before he became wrong and that the holiness movement developed largely because Methodism was headed the wrong direction.

[51]See also their New York Times op-ed at http://www. nytimes.com /2011/10/18/opinion/the-evangelical-rejection-of-reason.html?_r=2&

[52]Oden, *Requiem* (Nashville: Abingdon, 1995), 135.

The Case of Nathanael Burwash

At his death in 1918, Nathanael Burwash was the most influential Canadian Methodist. We remember him today primarily as the editor of Wesley's sermons, known as *Wesley Doctrinal Standards* (1881).

Burwash was born into a devout Methodist home. Like Wesley's mother, Susanna, Anne Burwash was devoted to the spiritual formation of her children. She catechized and prayed with her children. Nathanael was reared with a tender conscience. At thirteen he professed the knowledge that his sins were forgiven, although six years earlier he had gone forward desiring to be a Christian.

As a fourteen-year-old college student, revival swept through Victoria College. At any hour of the day prayer meetings were conducted, and the normal work of the students was almost completely suspended. Throughout his life, Burwash preached the witness of the Spirit.

It was during his senior year that Charles Darwin's *Origin of Species* was published. This influence began to penetrate the educational realm, and two basic ingredients of the old college curriculum came under attack — that God was Creator and that the Scriptures were completely reliable.

Robert John Taylor documented that two prominent Canadian scholars rejected Darwin's hypothesis, but two equally prominent scholars, including Burwash, embraced it. It became his agenda to reconcile religious faith and scientific thought.[53]

Burwash spent six years as a pastor before returning to the classroom. Ultimately he became chancellor of Canada's largest Methodist university. His lifelong goal was to defend the old Methodist traditions by utilizing the new tools of reason. Since science utilized the inductive method, theology

---

[53]Taylor, "The Darwinian Revolution: The Responses of Four Canadian Scholars," (PhD diss, McMaster University, 1976).

would also have to limit itself to inductive reasoning. Thus, Burwash produced his magnus opus in 1900, his two-volume *Manual of Christian Theology on the Inductive Method.*

By 1885 Burwash subscribed wholeheartedly to the theory of evolution, calling it "the most influential scientific doctrine of our time." By 1885-6, Burwash also began to teach that the early chapters of Genesis were not historical. The primary purpose of the account was to explain a religious truth, "a fundamental view of man in his moral relations and of the origin of sin and evil," rather than a doctrine of man's creation. By 1894, Victoria College was described as a" hot-bed of evolution."

Burwash also began teaching that the book of Isaiah was produced by two different authors writing at totally different times. He regularly came to the defense of his more liberal professors who were more pronounced in their embrace of higher criticism. He appealed to Wesley as one who utilized reason and was not as dogmatic as Calvin. As Burwash explained, "A man can be a Methodist today and believe far differently from what Methodists believed half a century ago." Thus, Wesley's notes and sermons could, in fact, be quoted in support of either a conservative view of the Bible or the more modern view.

In order to reconcile Methodist doctrine with modern philosophy and science, Burwash declared that the Methodist Articles of Religion spoke only of "the Sufficiency of the Holy Scriptures for Salvation." By 1910, the Conference approved the teaching of higher criticism, ending a twenty-year fight from conservatives. Burwash had been instrumental in defeating the more conservative voices. As long as biblical interpretation continued to emphasize the central doctrines of salvation, there was nothing to fear from "the modern view of the Bible."

Burwash was sympathetic toward those who felt that such issues were not practical and gave his blessing to one who left to join the Salvation Army, which was not concerned with such matters. But Burwash felt that the college needed academic freedom. He claimed his teaching was still the old Gospel but that the new understanding of its form expressed Methodist spirituality more clearly. "Piety had simply been updated."

Burwash continued to hold that "the inner assurance" was a guarantee that religious faith would be maintained in the face of any scientific challenge. Thus, he was perceived as the last bastion of a crumbling Christian faith against the onslaught of secularization. But as a theologian, he bore direct responsibility for defending those who were contributing to the decline of religious values and influence in Canadian society.

Burwash upheld repentance, forgiveness through the atonement, the witness of the Spirit, a life of holiness, and postmillennialism his entire life. He emphasized individual responsibility, moral perfectibility, the reliability of the senses, and the inevitability of progress. But in such a milieu, some of his students lost their faith and departed from the ministry. Others moved from his emphasis to a social gospel.

Through compartmentalized thinking, Burwash could affirm evolution and the faith of his childhood, but the next generation did not necessarily share his devout rearing, his intuitive certainty, and could not reconcile two contradictory authorities. Burwash was confident that science could be turned into "the handmaid of religion for our age." But when science attacked biblical revelation, the solution for Burwash was to adjust his interpretation of the Scriptures. The problem was not an inductive approach to Scripture, but the naïve acceptance of anti-Scriptural presuppositions.

Long before Albert Outler was writing about the Wesleyan quadrilateral,[54] Burwash emphasized four co-ordinate

---

[54]Outler later expressed regret that he coined the term because it had been so misconstrued. As Randy Maddox explained, Wesley had "a unilateral *rule* of Scripture within a trilateral *hermeneutic* of reason, tradition, and

authorities for doctrine: "the Apostolic Word," reason, tradition, and experience of "the inner light which is given to every true Christian." This paradigm allowed Burwash to embrace evolutionary thought and to retain his personal assurance of salvation.

He continued to preach and uphold in public the great Wesleyan themes, but in private worked toward an ecumenical union. He felt that all the denominations in Canada could be united under an inductive statement of faith. However, Calvinists continued to interpret it according to their presuppositions, and Arminians did the same.

His optimistic worldview interpreted the proceedings as an "inner oneness of the Spirit," but his biographer, Van Die, wrote that he "was finding it increasingly difficult to maintain the balance between the old and the new."[55] While Burwash devoted much energy to an ecumenical agenda, in his later years he grew silent about church union and spent his final years defending the Methodist tradition.

He began to remark that such "old-fashioned Methodist conversions" were becoming more rare at home. During the final five years of his life he became increasingly critical of developments within his denomination and within Canadian society. He began to call for revival, urging the formation of small holiness bands. "Better a lonely messenger of God without a church but baptized with the Holy Spirit than a worldly half dead church with great numbers and all worldly attractions," he exhorted. Increasingly he began to see himself as a "lonely messenger."

As pluralism and secularism moved into Canadian culture, his liberalism was only prepared to go so far. Thus, the

---

experience" [*Responsible Grace: John Wesley's Practical Theology* (Nashville: Abingdon, 1994), 46.

[55]Marguerite Van Die, *An Evangelical Mind: Nathanael Burwash and the Methodist Tradition in Canada, 1839-1918* (Montreal: McGill-Queen's University Press, 1989), 177.

next generation brushed past him as they kept pace with liberal trends which he could not accept.

By 1912 the Methodist denomination had committed itself to church union and his systematic theology had become dated. Burwash died before he could see the practical applications of evolutionary theory in the twentieth century. While Victoria University still exists as part of the federated University of Toronto, its evangelical influence has long since gone.

As they say, "history repeats itself." One only need to change the names, dates, and locations and this sketch could serve as an account of what is happening today within the Church of the Nazarene, as well as other denominations which left Methodism over these very issues. The results will be no better.

The Shift in Nazarene Theology

In 2009, the SW Indiana District submitted a resolution to the General Assembly to strengthen the Church of the Nazarene statement on Scripture. It was set aside for a four year study.

The "Report of the Scripture Study Committee to the Twenty-Eighth General Assembly" was presented June 19-28, 2013 in response to the resolution. The committee concluded,

> That it is not only unnecessary, but that it would be untrue to the Wesleyan tradition, incompatible with Wesleyan theology, and unwarranted by the Scriptures themselves, to add any assertion that the Scriptures are "inerrant throughout" not only in revealing the will of God for our salvation, but in determining the truth of any statement whatsoever. That would be to turn the Bible from the saving word of God into an almanac or encyclopedia. To say that the Scriptures are "the supreme authority on everything

the Scriptures teach" merely raises the question of what exactly the Scriptures teach, and there are numerous unsettled disputes among Christians (and even among Nazarenes) about that. To assert the complete detailed factual literal accuracy of every part of Scripture ('inerrant throughout') raises more problems than it solves and diverts people into unnecessary, distracting and futile disputes.[56]

To support this conclusion, they explained that the demand for complete detailed "inerrancy" originates from Calvinism and that this Calvinistic belief is the wrong way to assert the authority of the Scriptures. They strongly advised the amendment be rejected, stating that "Nazarenes are committed by the present Article IV to the sufficiency of Holy Scripture, its final authority in all matters of Christian faith and living, in doctrine and ethics. That is all we need to say."[57] Dr. Oord reported this as a rejection of "strict inerrancy."[58]

A. M. Hills, the first Nazarene to publish a systematic theology, denied that the Bible was absolutely inerrant.[59] But he concluded that in spite of errors, the Scripture was infallible.[60]

He did devote two chapters to the refutation of higher criticism and also rejected evolutionary Darwinism. But Donald Metz noted that the position of Hills on the Scripture

---

[56]"Report of the Scripture Study Committee to the Twenty-Eighth General Assembly," Thomas King, chairperson, p. 6.

[57]"Report of the Scripture Study Committee," p. 14.

[58]http://thomasjayoord.com/index.php/blog/archives/nazarenes_reject_strict_inerrancy/#.Ui-ypf-9Kc2

Dr. Oord is a professor at Northwest Nazarene University.

[59]A. M. Hills, *Fundamental Christian Theology*, (1931; rpt. Salem, OH: Schmul, 1980), 1:131.

[60]Hills, *Fundamental Christian Theology*, 1:134.

was a departure from the view of Wesley and the early Methodists.[61]

According to Metz, Hills introduced the idea of limited inspiration to Nazarene thought. Hills said the Bible "is infallible as regards the purpose for which it was written. It is infallible as the revelation of God's saving love in Christ to a wicked world. It infallibly guides all honest, and willing and seeking souls to Christ, to holiness and to heaven."[62]

Yet Hills originally held to full inerrancy. He originally wrote his theology in 1911 and sometime after 1915 he began to shift to a limited inerrancy position.[63] Paul Bassett revealed that the Nazarene Publishing House did not print Hills' theology because it was too liberal with respect to the authority and inspiration of Scripture.[64]

H. Orton Wiley did not publish the first volume of his theology until 1940, although it was commissioned in 1919. He defined "inspiration" as "the actuating energy of the Holy Spirit through which holy men were qualified to receive religious truth, and to communicate it to others without error."[65]

According to Richard S. Taylor, Wiley framed the statement in the creed of the Church of the Nazarene which includes the clause, "inerrantly revealing the will of God, concerning us in all things necessary to our salvation." This

---

[61]Donald S. Metz, *Some Critical Issues in the Church of the Nazarene* (Olathe, KS: Pioneer Press, 1993), 132-133. Metz was the founding academic dean of MidAmerica Nazarene University.

[62]Hills, *Fundamental Christian Theology*, 1:134.

[63]Daryl E. McCarthy, "Inerrancy in American Wesleyanism," in *Inerrancy and the Church*, John D. Hannah, ed. (Chicago: Moody, 1984), 305-308.

[64]Paul M. Bassett, "The Fundamentalist Leavening of the Holiness Movement, 1914-1940, The Church of the Nazarene: A Case Study," *Wesleyan Theological Journal* 13:1 (Spring 1978) 80.

[65]Wiley, *Christian Theology* (Kansas City: Beacon Hill, 1940), 1:169.

statement was not in the 1905 manual, but was added in 1928. It is claimed that Wiley deliberately articulated a moderate statement because he wanted "to leave elbow room in there."[66]

But Taylor insisted that this statement did not imply error in the Bible of any kind. "The objective was not to limit inerrancy but to exclude tradition."[67]

But Michael Lodahl holds that Wiley,

> Insured that the denomination would espouse the conviction that biblical authority is rooted in *soteriology*, or the doctrine of salvation. The implication is that Christians esteem the Bible not as an end in itself, but as a testimony to God's saving activity in the world through the people of Israel and then particularly, and finally, through Jesus Christ.[68]

The question, however, is whether Dr. Lodahl, writing in 2004, is projecting the theology of Rob Staples, which he articulated in the 1990s, to Wiley's theological influence in 1928. According to Lodahl,

> The fundamentalist approach was (and is) to read the Bible as a package of objective propositions that simply state the truth about everything they touch on. Wiley, at this critical juncture in the young history of the Church of the Nazarene, gently nudged the denomination in another direction. He

---

[66]This statement is also found in J. Kenneth Grider, *A Wesleyan-Holiness Theology* (Kansas City: Beacon Hill, 1994), 82.

[67]Richard S. Taylor, *Biblical Authority and Christian Faith* (Kansas City: Beacon Hill, 1980), 34-35.

[68]Michael Lodahl, *All Things Necessary to Our Salvation: The Hermeneutical and Theological Implications of the Article on the Holy Scriptures in the Manual of the Church of the Nazarene* (San Diego: Point Loma Press, 2004), 16.

> encouraged his fellow Nazarenes, instead, to approach the Holy Scriptures as having been inspired by God for the function of *revealing God's salvific will for God's people*, and that in this function the Scriptures do not err.[69]

Yet when Wiley is consulted, he repeatedly affirms biblical inerrancy, even concerning such historical facts as creation and the flood.[70] Wiley wrote, "Only as we are convinced that the writers were aided by a supernatural and divine influence, and this in such a manner as to be infallibly preserved from all error, can the sacred Scripture become a divine rule of faith and practice."[71]

Regarding this last statement of Wiley's, Thomas Oord wrote,

> In this quote, Wiley surprisingly claims the writers themselves – not the text – are "infallibly preserved from all error." This is a strong claim, given that he rejects mechanical/dictation theories of inspiration! . . . A few lines in these long chapters sound like Wiley affirms absolute textual inerrancy. He says, for instance, that "God so guides those chosen as the organs of revelation that their writings are kept free from error" (171). While statements about the inerrancy of the text are rare, and the casual reader might conclude that Wiley believed in absolute textual inerrancy. In the final segment of his long discussion of revelation, however, Wiley addresses the "integrity of the Scriptures." By this, he means, the Bible has been "kept intact and free from essen-

---

[69]Lodahl, *All Things Necessary to Our Salvation*, 30.

[70]Wiley, *Christian Theology*, 1:172-173; see also 1:167.

[71]Wiley, *Christian Theology*, 1:173.

> tial error, so that we may be assured of the truth originally given by the inspired authors" (212). Notice that Wiley inserts the word "essential" in this sentence. The Bible is free from "essential" error. In the same discussion, he writes, "No proof has ever yet been furnished of essential alterations" (212). He even makes the bold claim that proof of essential alterations could never be found in the future! Of course, there is an important difference between saying the Bible has no "essential" errors and saying the Bible has no errors at all. It's the difference between some and none.

But Oord missed Wiley's point. Wiley affirmed the full inerrancy of the inspiration process, but allowed that there could be some nonessential error in the preservation of the manuscript texts.

As Oord reaches his conclusion, he also seems to realize that while he admired Wiley, Wiley is much more conservative. Therefore, Oord makes this disclaimer,

> My conclusion is that Wiley's basic intuitions are still helpful. He doesn't give the last word – or even the first word, for that matter – on how we ought to think about the Bible. And contemporary Christians must listen closely to the best biblical and theological scholars today.[72]

While Oord expresses surprise that Wiley affirmed inerrancy since he rejected mechanical/dictations theories, the two concepts are not necessarily connected. In his book affirming inerrancy, Stewart Custer declared concerning the dictation

---

[72]http://thomasjayoord.com/index.php/blog/archives/wiley_on_the_bible/

theory, “Almost all conservatives reject this theory.”[73]

Daryl McCarthy has traced the declarations of the Church of the Nazarene over its first twenty years (1908-1928) and has determined that the full inerrancy of Scripture was a frequent theme.[74] As late as 1948 Ross Price wrote in the *Herald of Holiness*,

> Our Lord, in this argument, assumed the absolute truth of the Scripture, and its changeless, indestructible authority. . . . The Bible is correct astronomically, geologically, historically, medically, botanically, zoologically. meterologically, prophetically, and spiritually. It is the final court of appeals on matters of faith and practice.[75]

In 1960 W. T. Purkiser asked, “Can we really have revelation without a Bible which is doctrinally inerrant and factually trustworthy?” While this is the right question, after eleven pages the answer is still unclear. Purkiser seemed to be influenced by neo-orthodoxy and refers to the Bible as “a record of revelation.”[76]

In 1978 the *Convention Herald*, published by the Inter-Church Holiness Convention, contained a series of editorials

---

[73]Custer, Does Inspiration Demand Inerrancy? (Nutley, NJ: Craig Press, 1968), 10.

[74]McCarthy, “Inerrancy in American Wesleyanism,” 295-305.

[75]Price, “The Immutability of the Scriptures (John 10:35),” *Herald of Holiness* (29 Nov 1948) 670-671. Dr. Price was a professor at Pasadena Nazarene College.

[76]Purkiser, *Exploring Our Christian Faith*, Revised Edition (Kansas City: Beacon, 1978), 59-70. Dr. Purkiser was president of Pasadena Nazarene College from 1948-1957. He later served as editor of the *Herald of Holiness* for fifteen years.

expressing concern over the teaching of J. Kenneth Grider.[77] H. E. Schmul published a letter from Grider stating, "I have never taught either in a class session or in any publication either that the Bible autographs were in error of any kind whatever, or that Christ erred in any way whatever."[78]

However, in Grider's 1994 theology, *A Wesleyan-Holiness Theology*, he refused to take a position that the Bible is totally without error. Grider then carried his premise to a dangerous conclusion. Based on his view of the written Word, he then argued that "Christ was sinless, not that He was totally errorless on unimportant matters."[79] These were the very teachings of Grider over which Schmul had expressed concern.

In 1979 Harold Lindsell warned that the Church of the Nazarene had been deeply infiltrated by an errancy view, which was believed and taught in most, if not all of its educational institutions. Lindsell concluded that "a house divided against itself cannot stand. The Church of the Nazarene should make plain which of the two incompatible viewpoints represents the church and its people."[80]

H. Ray Dunning rejected the doctrine of inerrancy in his

---

[77]Schmul, "The Inerrancy Issue," *Convention Herald* 32:2 (Feb 1978) 2; Schmul, "Editorial," *Convention Herald* 32:3 (March 1978) 2; Schmul, "Inerrancy Fallout," *Convention Herald* 32:8 (Aug 1978) 2-3; Schmul, "Inerrancy vs. Authority," *Convention Herald* 32:9 (Sept 1978) 2-3. See also Schmul's letter to me, 26 Feb 1979.

[78]Schmul, "Inerrancy Fallout," *Convention Herald* 32:8 (Aug 1978) 2-3.

[79]Grider, *A Wesleyan-Holiness Theology*, 75-79. Dr. Grider was a professor at Nazarene Theological Seminary for thirty-eight years.

[80]Lindsell, *The Bible in the Balance* (Grand Rapids: Zondervan, 1979), 107-110.

1988 theology.[81] Dunning concluded,

> While some Nazarenes interpret [the article of faith in the *Manual of the Church of the Nazarene*] to imply full authority in the broadest sense . . . other Nazarene sources allow a more restricted interpretation, defining it as extending to the whole canon; in terms of the content of Scripture, to the soteriological aspects of the Bible, that is, it holds that the way of salvation set forth in Scripture is completely reliable and dependable.[82]

The *Beacon Dictionary of Theology*, published by the Nazarene Beacon Hill Press in 1983 affirmed inerrancy. George Allen Turner wrote that "inerrancy" and "infallible" were synonymous terms. Both carry the concept of "without mistake."[83]

However, the new 2013 *Global Wesleyan Dictionary of Theology*, published thirty years later by the same press, declares that Wesleyans accept the Reformation principle of Scripture only. But we are also told that authority is not based on the Bible's very words. Apparently, biblical authority is in process within the Church and through the Spirit.

The assumption of soteriological inerrancy permeates the whole dictionary. "Wesleyans reject using Scripture as a textbook for biology, anthropology, cosmology, physics, or

---

[81]Dunning, *Grace, Faith, and Holiness* (Kansas City: Beacon Hill, 1988), 60-61. Dr. Dunning was a professor at Trevecca Nazarene University from 1964-1995.

[82]Dunning, *Grace, Faith, and Holiness*, 72.

[83]Turner, "Biblical Inerrancy," *Beacon Dictionary of Theology* (Kansas City: Beacon Hill, 1983), 75.

geography."[84] We are assured that Wesleyans understand evolution to be compatible with Christian theology. "Although fundamentalists . . . understand evolution to be incompatible with Christian theology, this is not the case for a Wesleyan understanding of God."[85]

The article on biblicism/bibliolary was a reaction against 24-hour days of creation and biblical inerrancy, as well as an accusation that we worship the Bible. Elsewhere we are told that Wesleyans avoid the extreme of biblical fundamentalism in which the Bible's words are thought to be dictated by God. However, we are assured that every type of biblical criticism is a legitimate tool for Wesleyan scholars.

By 1998, Rob Staples articulated what was becoming the official position of the Church of the Nazarene. He was the first person to use the term "soteriological inerrancy."[86]

What is Soteriological Inerrancy?

In his monthly column "Words of Faith" for *Herald of Holiness*, Rob Staples wrote on "Inerrancy" in June 1998. He rejected "epistemological inerrancy" and opted for "soteriological inerrancy."

Epistemology deals with the nature, limits, and validity of knowledge. The most basic question in theology is, "What is the source of knowledge?" Only after the source of knowledge and truth has been established as reliable, can we go on to discuss other matters, such as salvation. Since the Bible is epistemologically inerrant, everything it says on any subject

---

[84]Kent Brower, "Wesleyan Approach to Scripture," *Global Wesleyan Dictionary of Theology*, Al Truesdale, ed. (Kansas City: Beacon Hill, 2013), 489.

[85]Darrel Falk, "Evolution/Evolutionary Biology," *Global Wesleyan Dictionary*, 191.

[86]Staples letter to Vic Reasoner, 26 October 1998. Dr. Staples was a professor at Nazarene Theological Seminary for twenty-two years.

must be true, and we can trust its message of salvation.

But Staples rejected this approach, declaring that Wesleyan theology works differently. For Wesleyanism, Staples said the most basic theological question is, "What must I do to be saved?" "In Wesleyan theology, salvation *is* truth. Truth is determined by what salvation is, not the other way around."

If there are many answers to the question, "What must I do to be saved?" Why would we regard the biblical answer as inerrant and reject the answers of tradition, reason, experience, and even other religions?

Staples offers no support for his statement that "salvation is truth." We are expected to accept this paradigm on the authority of Staples. He does not demonstrate that Wesley ever held such an epistemology.

In fact, Wesley wrote that the foundation of true religion stands upon the oracles of God, and the Apostles' Creed is a beautiful summary of the essential truths contained in Scripture.[87] Yet the Apostles' Creed deals with more than salvific truth. It affirms God as Creator and even affirms the historical time frame of the passion of Jesus Christ. Certainly there is nothing salvific about Pontius Pilate. Yet many congregations in the Methodist tradition affirm that historical reality every Sunday.

To support his position, Staples quoted John Wesley's statement, "I want to know one thing, the way to heaven; how to land safe on that happy shore." Staples quoted from Wesley's preface to his sermons. Yet in this preface Wesley continued,

> God himself has condescended to teach the way: for this very end he came from heaven. He hath written it down in a book. O give me that book! At any price give me the Book of God! I have it. Here is knowl-

---

[87]Wesley, "The Case of Reason Impartially Considered," Sermon #70, 1.6.

> edge enough for me. Let me be *homo unius libri* [a man of one book].

Does it matter whether this Book is inerrant? Does revelation from an omniscient God demand inerrancy? Staples dismissed full inerrancy by arguing that all that matters is salvation. But one cannot argue that the "one thing" Wesley wanted to know was only salvation any more than one can argue that Wesley only read one book.

Ironically, Staples then makes this disclaimer,

> This does not mean that we can separate the Bible's teaching about salvation from its statements about other matters and claim that the latter may contain errors, while those texts that speak of salvation do not. That would be a precarious position. Who is to decide how to separate the two kinds of texts? Who is to say whether a text does, or does not, relate to salvation?[88]

Staples has just pinpointed the weakness of his own position. Klug explained,

> If scholars themselves determine what the Word or "message" is, then plainly they are responsible for establishing whatever is canonical about the canon. Obviously this can be a very subjective exercise. With each exegete or Bible scholar conceiving it to be his task to locate the "canon in the canon," there can be no guarantee of that message, or the Word.[89]

---

[88]Staples, "Inerrancy," *Herald of Holiness* (June 1998) 5. This became part of Staples, *Words of Faith* (Kansas City: Beacon Hill, 2001), 21-22.

[89]Eugene F. Klug, "Foreword," in Gerhard Maier, *The End of the Historical-Critical Method* (1977; rpt. Eugene, OR: Wipf & Stock, 2001), 9.

In the Fall 1998 issue of *The Arminian Magazine*, I wrote a short article expressing my concerns with soteriological inerrancy, as articulated by Dr. Staples.[90] I then received a four-page letter from Dr. Staples. His main concern was that I did not understand the difference between "limited inerrancy" and "soteriological inerrancy."[91]

According to Staples soteriological inerrancy is expressed in the sentence, "The entire Bible is inerrant for salvation." Limited inerrancy is expressed in the sentence, "The parts of the Bible that deal with salvation are inerrant while the other parts may contain errors." Staples gave me a second example of limited inerrancy, "The Bible is inerrant only in those parts that deal with salvation."

Staples wrote,

> I have never yet met a Fundamentalist who did not try to tar the "soteriological inerrantists" with the "limited inerrantist" brush, even when the difference is as obvious as the nose on my face.[92]

Perhaps that is because both terms amount to the same thing.

As I compare the two positions, the difference I see is that the first statement expresses only the positive proposition. It does not deal with the negative implications. But if the entire Bible is inerrant *only* for salvation, then it seems that soteriological inerrancy is also limited inerrancy. I can only

---

[90]Reasoner, "Defending Biblical Inerrancy," *The Arminian Magazine* 16:2 (Fall 1998) 6-8.

[91]At one point in the letter Staples accused me of libel in misrepresentation of his position. Because that is a serious allegation, I submitted myself to the judgment of my peers. After reading both sides, their conclusion was that the dog which yelps is the one that got hit.

[92]Staples letter to Vic Reasoner, 26 October 1998.

conclude that Staples does not accept full inerrancy when he says in his article on inerrancy that divisiveness occurs whenever the issue of inerrancy "has reared it's ugly head."

It seems that the difference between soteriological inerrancy and limited inerrancy is that in the first case you merely state the positive proposition and hope that no one asks about the negative implications. If they do ask, you then claim you are being misunderstood. In spite of semantic gymnastics, there seems to be no practical difference between soteriological and limited inerrancy.

This reminds me of the Calvinists who uphold limited election, but cry "foul" if you try to pin "double predestination" on them. They want to affirm the position that God elects some to salvation, but they reject the logical corollary that the non-elect are thus predestined to damnation.

In his letter Staples declared, "I have never claimed that there were errors (either minor or major) in the Scriptures. I have no proof that such exists." But Staples continued to say that if there were, he would either have to throw away his faith in Scripture and hence in salvation or explain away the discrepancies. Staples continued, "We true Wesleyans do not have to worry about the former, nor waste time and effort on the latter." Staples gave this illustration,

> When I lived in the San Francisco area, years ago, I often crossed the Golden Gate Bridge. I never questioned the structure of the bridge. I never wondered if there were some rusty bolts or weak cables in the structure, or if the sea water might have weakened the piers underneath. Now there may have been some weaknesses, but I had no proof of such, although I did see them painting the structure from time to time, to prevent rust. But even if such weaknesses existed, the purpose of the bridge, and my purpose in crossing it, were to get me to the other

side. I trusted the engineers and the inspectors to keep it safe for cars to cross. If I had known there was a rusty bolt on the bridge, or one hairline crack in one of the girders, and had been a "fundamentalist motorist" (to coin a term) I would have had to refuse to cross the bridge, considering it unreliable. If a few minor defects had shown up (and I never knew about it if they did) it would not have affected my determination to get to the other side, and it did not cause me to refuse to use the bridge for the crossing. Thus the bridge was perfect, infallible, ("inerrant"), for the purpose for which it was built. And that applies to the whole bridge, not just to the "transportational" (read "salvational") parts of it. The bridge, the whole bridge, not just parts of it, not just the pavement on which my tires rolled, was absolutely inerrant for getting me to the other side.[93]

In 2006, Dr. Staples sent me an email stating that he had been asked to collect his papers for the Nazarene Archives. In the process he came across his 1998 letter to me. After showing that letter to a number of people, their conclusion was that his letter contained the best exposition of the Wesleyan view of Scripture they had ever seen because it "clearly shows how we differ from both Liberals and Fundamentalists."

Staples closed, "I have you to thank for eliciting that letter out of me, so I am writing to do so now, belatedly as it may be."[94] And yet I think his logic is flawed. To cross a bridge without the knowledge that it contains structural damage is presumption. Would Staples cross the same bridge if he knew it was in a weakened condition? Bridges can collapse.

On August 1, 2007, the I-35W Mississippi River bridge

---

[93]Staples letter to Vic Reasoner, 26 October 1998.

[94]Rob L. Staples, "On Scripture," email 15 October 2006.

(officially known as Bridge 9340) was an eight-lane, steel truss arch bridge that carried Interstate 35W across the Mississippi River in Minneapolis. During the evening rush hour it suddenly collapsed, killing 13 people and injuring 145. The bridge was Minnesota's fifth busiest, carrying 140,000 vehicles daily. The National Transportation Safety Board cited a design flaw as the likely cause of the collapse.

Furthermore, Staples' analogy of an inanimate, decaying bridge is inadequate. Scripture was not only God-breathed, but that God-breathing is ongoing as God continues to speak through his written Word. Is modern Wesleyanism afraid that science will discredit the Scriptures? If the Bible is described in terms of a bridge, then the good news is that it is solid and in no danger of collapse.

Faith can also collapse when it is undermined. One of my best friends attended one of the largest evangelical Wesleyan seminaries, but one that no longer holds to inerrancy. I first met him in 1993. He had experienced a radical deliverance from sin and showed great potential. We even roomed together at Wesleyan Theological Society meetings. He preached for me and I preached for him. But his professors at seminary gradually eroded his confidence in the Scriptures.

He was taught that while the Bible did have mistakes, since it was canonized by the Church it was authoritative. He was told that we should begin with what we have and seek to interpret it for today. While they believe the document is flawed, its authority rests on the fact that it is accepted by the community of faith.

But by 1998, my friend sent me an email stating,

> The more I have studied the more I have come to believe that the Bible is not "inspired" or "God-breathed" or the "Word of God." It seems to me that Christianity is just another false religion, and that the Bible is just another attempt at a holy book. I

> have been agnostic for about the last two years. . . . I have studied this issue very carefully, and I cannot believe in the Bible or Christianity with what I know about it now. I never imagined that this would happen to me.[95]

When told that the "bridge had cracks in it," he did not keep on driving toward heaven — even though the Church told him not to worry. He turned back and became apostate.

The doctrine of soteriological inerrancy is an errant position for three basic reasons.

1. It redefines inerrancy.

Those who affirm biblical inerrancy hold that the Bible is true in all that it affirms. The position of the International Conference of Biblical Inerrancy states,

> Inerrancy means that when all facts are known, the Scriptures in their original autographs and properly interpreted will be shown to be wholly true in everything that they affirm, whether that has to do with doctrine or morality, or with the social, physical, or life sciences.[96]

Those who say they hold to soteriological inerrancy hold that the Bible is true when it deals with salvation. While they continue to use the same term, they have redefined and limited its meaning. While their constituency hears the familiar word "inerrancy," they do not realize the accepted definition of the term has been rejected.

---

[95]Private email, 23 April 1998.

[96]Paul D. Feinberg, "The Meaning of Inerrancy," in *Inerrancy*, Norman L. Geisler, ed. (Grand Rapids: Zondervan), 294.

2. It is a form of reductionism.

To limit the Creator to the domain of "religion" destroys the unity between nature and grace. God is sovereign over every sphere of life and cannot be confined to matters of salvation only. The old Manichean world view held that the spiritual world was good while the material world was evil. But the Christian world view is that everything is to be brought under the lordship of Christ. Therefore, we reject a dualism which holds to an inspiration which applies only to salvation. Historically, even the Church of the Nazarene has held to plenary or full inspiration.

In the field of apologetics, history, nature, prophecy, and miracles have been used to confirm Scripture. If the record is not accurate at these points, how do we know it is reliable when dealing with salvation? What the Nazarene theologians are advocating amounts to compartmentalized revelation. How can the Bible be trustworthy in one area but not in other areas? Partial trustworthiness makes as much sense as a partial pregnancy.

The dominion mandate of Genesis 1:26-28 legitimizes science, technology, commerce, government, education, the arts, and culture. Also implied in our vocation is a concern with ecology and the environment. The lordship of Christ cannot be reduced to the saving of souls. As Abraham Kuyper declared in his 1880 inaugural address at the Free University of Amsterdam, "There is not a square inch in the whole domain of our human existence over which Christ, who is Sovereign over all, does not cry: 'Mine!'"

3. It leads to limited authority.

A doctrine of limited inerrancy weakens the authority of Scripture. Someone must determine for us when the Bible is inerrant and when it is not. If Scripture is not always infallible, then an infallible authority must tell us when we can trust Scripture. Thus, by necessity there must be a final authority. In the case of the limited authority of Scripture, our ultimate authority becomes the final verdict of the scholars.

After Dr. Staples published his column on "Inerrancy," the following month he wrote on "Authority." He concluded that the final religious authority for Christians is neither Scripture, tradition, reason, nor experience. He declared the gospel is our final authority in matters of faith and practice, and the gospel is Jesus Christ.[97] Yet we would know nothing about Jesus Christ or his gospel unless God had written it down in a book. Unless the Scriptures are accepted as our final authority (a major theme of the Protestant reformation), the content of the gospel can be changed. And in many cases today the gospel is being redefined.

W. B. Pope expressed his strong conviction that "this book, or library of books, is the record of that Providential government for the sake of which the world exists" and that "we may be sure that is will not be contradicted in fundamental points by anything that the records of nature, or the authentic annals of history, will disclose."[98] There are reasonable explanations to apparent contradictions which are stronger than the basis of the supposed doubt.[99] Those who hold to a high view of inspiration will find that most of our problems are matters of hermeneutics. I approach the text with the assumption that God knew what he was saying, but the problem is with my limited understanding.

J. B. Phillips wrote that although he did not hold fundamentalist views on inspiration he was continually struck by the

---

[97]Staples, "Authority," *Herald of Holiness* (July 1998) 6.

[98]Pope, *Compendium*, 1:190.

[99]This is the case with Thomas Jay Oord's list of "mistakes." <http://thomasjayoord.com/index.php/blog/archives/problems_with_biblical_inerrancy/>

living quality of the material he was translating. He said he "felt rather like an electrician rewiring an ancient house without being able to 'turn the mains off.'"[100] This is because of the power of the Word. It is the revelation of God and is not more in danger of collapse than God himself.

However, the ultimate issue for evangelical Wesleyans is not inerrancy. It is authority. Authority is the logical conclusion of divine inspiration. The purpose of inspiration was to convey truth. God is the source of all truth; truth without error. Therefore, inspiration demands inerrancy. If the Bible contains errors, its authority is limited. But if the work of the Holy Spirit was to transmit revelation to the human authors and to superintend their writings, then a Bible with historical and scientific errors reflects on the capability of the Holy Spirit.

It also implies that only a magisterium of intellectual elite are equipped to determine what parts of Scripture are correct. Thus, authority is an inescapable concept. The only question up for debate regards who or what will be our final authority. According to William Abraham,

> For Wesley, Scripture was the Word of God, dictated by God, authored by God even as it was written by human authors. To speak of Scripture was to speak of God; more accurately, it was to speak aptly and rightly of God, for Scripture gives us access to God. More abruptly, to refer to Scripture was to refer to the foundations of theology, the touchstone of theology; to invoke Scripture was to speak from and for God; it was to exercise the vocation of the theologian.[101]

---

[100]Phillips, *Letters to Young Churches* (New York: Macmillan, 1947), xii.

[101]Abraham, "The Future of Scripture: In Search of a Theology of Scripture," *Wesleyan Theological Journal* 46:1 (Spring 2011) 11.

While Abraham proceeds to reject this approach as a dead-end, the question is how much of Wesleyan theology can be discarded while still remaining "Wesleyan."

Francis Schaeffer warned that the rejection of inerrancy leads to a "slippery slope" which results in a latitudinarianism concerning the Bible.[102] While Dr. Staples claimed he had never taught that there were errors in the Bible, the next generation of Nazarene theologians have carried the doctrine of Staples to its logical conclusion.

In his book *The Story of God*, Michael Lodahl teaches,

> In many ways, it's the same way anyone's story gets told — except that this is a very old story, told over a considerable length of time with many tellers, twists, and complications, and with a rather unobtrusive main Character (God) who seems not to be overly concerned that we get the Story "just right" in every detail.[103]

I published an article which illustrated the fallacy of soteriological inerrancy by comparing the Word of God to bottled water. Those who hold to limited inerrancy basically claim the water is pure even if the bottle is not clean. The author proposed a label on the bottled water which read,

> We are not concerned with the scientific composition of the bottle itself. Furthermore, we are unsure of the historical facts regarding the handling of this bottle, and may have been misinformed as to its

---

[102]Schaeffer, "Foreword," *The Foundation of Biblical Authority*, James Montgomery Boice, ed. (Grand Rapids: Zondervan, 1978), 18. In *The Great Evangelical Disaster*, Schaeffer called the inerrancy and full authority of Scripture a watershed issue (Westchester, IL: Crossway, 1984), 44.

[103]Lodahl, *The Story of God* (Kansas City: Beacon Hill, 1994), 16.

> origin. Nevertheless, we insure you its contents are pure.[104]

> In response to this article, Michael Lodahl wrote me,

> Indeed, Genesis 2 states that the human being (*adam*) was God-breathed (v. 7), but surely this did not entail, let alone necessitate, the human's infallibility. Adam, inbreathed by God, nonetheless fell into disobedience. For that matter, Psalm 104:29-30 celebrates the perhaps surprising idea that all creatures, not just humans, are God-breathed. These texts would suggest to us that to be "God-breathed" is to be alive, living and breathing, sharing in the generously-bestowed life of God - but having precious little to do with absolute inerrancy in all matters.[105]

His colleague at Point Loma published an open letter in the Spring of 2009. In it C. S. Cowles declared that all communication may be essentially true, even if it contains incidental errors. He then argued that if this were not the case

> I would have to stop talking to my family and friends, listening to sermons and Garrison Keillor's fictional Lake Wobegon stories, and cease reading all newspapers, magazines, books, and letters from my grandchildren.

This all seems rather over the top. I love to get mail from my grandson. However, his writing is not infallible because he

---

[104]Jonathan A. Staniforth, "Inerrancy and the Wesleyan Tradition," *The Arminian Magazine* 27:1 (Spring 2009) 1-4.

[105]Lodahl, "Rejoinder," email 12 October 2010.

does not write under the direct inspiration of the Holy Spirit. There is a difference. In 1885, Methodist theologian Milton S. Terry explained,

> As for alleged discrepancies, contradictions, and errors of the Bible, we deny that any real errors can be shown. But our doctrine of divine inspiration is compatible with incorrect spelling, involved rhetoric, imperfect grammar, and inelegant language [at least by current standards].[106]

But Cowles continues to argue that while maps are distorted, they still lead us to our destination. Of course, that presumes we know how to read a map. I have met many people who could not! I still think the problem is with the reader, not the One who inspired our roadmap to heaven.

Then Cowles states that "inerrant" is a negative, nonbiblical, and misleading word, that inerrancy is alien to the contents of the Scriptures themselves, and that the Bible is not only divine but human — very human indeed. Here he accuses inerrantists of Gnosticism, by claiming that we deny the human element of the Scriptures, just as the early Gnostics denied that Christ was human. According to Cowles the result is that the robots who take dictation from God are like Stepford wives or New Age Channelers.

Cowles continues by asserting that inerrantists do not really believe that the Bible is inerrant because we recognize that it lacks modern technical precision, irregularities of grammar or spelling, observational descriptions of nature, the reporting of falsehoods, the use of hyperbole and round numbers, the topical arrangements of material, variant selections of material in parallel accounts, or the use of free citations.

---

[106]Terry, *Biblical Hermeneutics*, 148-149. Terry also declared, "We see no good reason for denying that the divine guidance extended to all parts and forms of the record" [p. 143].

Cowles accuses inerrantists of engaging in blatant double-speak which is misleading at best and dishonest at worst, but I don't see the problem. Cowles has argued for human freedom in the process of inspiration. Now he seems to deny that the Holy Spirit has the freedom to edit his own words as he sees fit.[107] Cowles is attacking his own strawman.

Article 8 of the 1978 Chicago Statement on Biblical Inerrancy stated,

> *WE DENY* that it is proper to evaluate Scripture according to standards of truth and error that are alien to its usage or purpose. We further deny that inerrancy is negated by Biblical phenomena such as a lack of modern technical precision, irregularities of grammar or spelling, observational descriptions of nature, the reporting of falsehoods, the use of hyperbole and round numbers, the topical arrangement of material, variant selections of material in parallel accounts, or the use of free citations.

It is generally agreed that inspiration is a divine/human endeavor. But why cannot we agree that the Holy Spirit is able to superintend the process, without bypassing their personalities, so that fallible men wrote an infallible Book?

But Cowles continues. He declares that because we do not obey Old Testament laws which require capital punishment for those who pick up sticks on the Sabbath, that we are not interpreting every part of Scripture as authoritative.

Then he declares that inerrancy encourages the atomization and abuse of Scripture. And I grant that Bible-believing preachers have made some rather amusing interpretive mistakes. But this same accusation could also be directed at those

---

[107]This concept is explained by Greg L. Bahnsen, "The Inerrancy of the Autographa," in *Inerrancy*, Geisler, ed, 170-171.

who uphold higher criticism, except that the results have often been tragic.

Yet Cowles claims that inerrancy distorts the very revelation of the God it seeks to protect. That's an odd proposition. We teach that inerrancy guarantees the accuracy of divine revelation.

Cowles then closes with the assertion that to absolutize the words of Scripture is to relativize Jesus. But he has created a false dilemma. Cowles declares that Jesus is our final authority not only in matters of faith and salvation but in determining the true nature of God. Where would I go to find the teachings of Jesus? Would they be found in an errant text? Or would we rely on a "Jesus Seminar" to vote on what Jesus really said? Their "five gospels" are one big hole with no cheese. Cowles declares that he reads the Scripture through a Christological lens, but I think he missed the words of Jesus in Matthew 5:18.[108]

In the newest Nazarene systematic theology, Samuel Powell, also at Point Loma, attempted to write an introductory level, consensus theology from a Wesleyan perspective. In it he wrote,

> Protestants differed from the medieval Church in seeing only the Bible as the product of the Spirit's inspiration. Creeds, customs, and theologians, they argued, were human and therefore, unlike the Bible, liable to error. The Bible, being inspired, fully,

---

[108]C. S. Cowles, "Scriptural Inerrancy? 'Behold, I Show You A More Excellent Way,'" An Open Letter, Spring, 2009, Point Loma Nazarene University.<www.naznet.com/inerrant.htm>or <www2.pointloma.edu/sites/default/files/filemanager/Wesleyan_Center/excellent-way.pdf>

Dr. Cowles is a professor at Point Loma Nazarene University.

accurately, and without error reveals the will of God.[109]

When I wrote Dr. Powell to ask what he meant by this statement he replied,

> I'm broadly sympathetic with what is often referred to as soteriological inerrancy, although I confess this is an area of theology in which I haven't done all my homework. . . . I can't convince myself that the Bible is a reliable source of scientific knowledge about the world — I just don't think this sort of knowledge was of much interest to the biblical writers and their communities. . . . At the same time, I am far from making scientific knowledge the measure of revelation and biblical interpretations. It's important to recognize the limitations of scientific knowledge. . . . The view I'm comfortable with these days is that the Bible is true in everything it affirms, even in its affirmations about the natural world, but that it views things and events according to their relation to God. So, the Bible makes some affirmations about the natural world that differ from the conclusions of the sciences, but those affirmations are still true because the biblical writers are portraying things, not according to their relation to natural laws but instead according to their relation to God.[110]

---

[109]Powell, *Discovering our Christian Faith* (Kansas City: Beacon Hill, 2008), 275.

[110]Powell email to Vic Reasoner, 6 January 2010. See Powell's defense of evolution <http://exploringevolution.com/essays/2013/08/12/why-i-believe/#.UoKWB42A3IV>

While I appreciate his candor, I am concerned that this view creates separate categories of truth. Thus, the Bible is true when it speaks of salvation, but not necessarily of history or science. The doctrines of creation cannot be divorced from the gospel of Jesus Christ since the teachings of Genesis are foundational to the gospel. Revelation 14:6-7 connects the preaching of the everlasting gospel with a call to worship the One who made heaven and earth, the sea and the fountains of waters. According to Colossians 1:16 the Christ who came to save us, was the very one who first created us. In Acts 14:15-17 and 17:23-28, Paul began his gospel message with the Creator.

In stating the official position of the Church of the Nazarene, Dr. Paul Cunningham wrote on behalf of the general superintendents,

> Wesleyans believe that Scripture accurately (inerrantly) communicates to us God's character ultimately revealed in Christ, the true nature of reality/our situation and God's plan for our salvation. The assurance of inerrancy points to God's revelation for our salvation in the broad sense. The point is salvation, not information. Though it should be said, "What is necessary for our salvation" should not be reduced to a narrow category of knowledge. An understanding of inerrancy that is focused on the literal accuracy of data is misdirected in a quite modern direction. It reflects a western scientific understanding of truth and language that is inadequate for biblical (and Christian) notions of truth.
>
> We realize there are many variations within the manuscripts of the Old and New Testaments. Our view on the inerrancy of Scripture does not apply to geography, science, mathematics, or historical statements. The Bible's soteriological message does not

embrace the scope of these other areas of human knowledge. However, we do not believe the God-inspired writers taught us any error on doctrine or practice — the real purpose of Scripture.[111]

The February 10-12, 2011 conference at Northwest Nazarene University, "The Bible Tells Me So" affirmed,

> The Bible is inerrant in what it does: the Spirit is at work revealing through human words the character and purposes of God to redeem, in Christ, all creation.[112]

Yet the chairperson, Thomas Oord, also posted a blog in which he identifies ten errors in the Bible.[113]

What Has Happened in Modern Wesleyan Theology?

There has been a major shift within the Wesleyan Theological Society concerning its position on inerrancy. In the first issue of the *Wesleyan Theological Journal*, Kenneth Geiger, former president of the National Holiness Association, wrote that the inerrancy of the original autographs of Scripture was the official position of the National Holiness Association and

---

[111]Paul Cunningham email to Jason R. Bjerke, 2 June 2009.

[112]http://thomasjayord.com/index/php/blog/archives/bible_conference_wrap-up/ Statement three of the Consensus Statement

[113]http://thomasjayoord.com/index.php/blog/archives/problems_with_biblical_inerrancy/

It is not my purpose to resolve each "error." A good study Bible can provide plausible answers. The question is whether we are looking for an answer or an error. We tend to find that for which we are looking. As a pastor/teacher my task is to strengthen faith, not tear it down. While the Bible does contain some things which are hard to understand, those who twist or distort these words to so to their own destruction (2 Peter 3:16).

"quite uniformly, the view of Wesleyan-Arminians everywhere."[114]

In its first four journals, the doctrinal position of the Wesleyan Theological Society stated that the Old and New Testaments were inerrant in the originals. This statement no longer appeared after 1969. However at least nine Wesleyan scholars signed the Chicago Statement on Biblical Inerrancy on January 1, 1979: Allan Coppedge, Wilbur T. Dayton, Ralph Earle, Eldon R. Fuhrman, Dennis F. Kinlaw, Daryl McCarthy, James Earl Massey, A. Skevington Wood, and Laurence W. Wood.[115]

The last *Wesleyan Theological Journal* article in support of biblical inerrancy appeared in 1981.[116] In 1984, Kenneth Grider expressed the hope that as the Wesleyan Theological Society began its next twenty years that it would do its homework and not accept the agenda of Calvinistic evangelicalism.[117] Since then the doctrine of biblical inerrancy has been labeled as anachronistic to Wesley's day, Calvinistic, and a fundamentalist doctrine.

It is anachronistic to claim that John Wesley would or would not have been in agreement with the 1978 Chicago

---

[114]Geiger,"The Biblical Basis for the Doctrine of Holiness," *Wesleyan Theological Journal* 1:1 (Spring 1966) 43. Much earlier Henry C. Sheldon concluded that American Methodist began with a high view of inspiration which affirmed inerrancy ["Changes in Theology Among American Methodists," *The American Journal of Theology* 10 (1906) 32.

[115]Geisler and Roach, *Defending Inerrancy*, 346-348. All except Earle and Skevington Wood have been published in the *Wesleyan Theological Journal.*

[116]Daryl McCarthy, "Early Wesleyan Views of Scripture," *Wesleyan Theological Journal* 16:2 (Fall 1981) 95-105. In 1998 Oden described a great gulf between the Evangelical Theological Society and the Wesleyan Theological Society ["The Real Reformers are Traditionalists," *Christianity Today* 42:2 (9 February 1998) 46].

[117]Grider, "Wesleyanism and the Inerrancy Issue," *Wesleyan Theological Journal* 19:2 (Fall 1984) 60.

Statement on Biblical Inerrancy. However, Wesley did declare, "Nay, if there be any mistakes in the Bible there may as well be a thousand. If there be one falsehood in that book, it did not come from the God of truth."[118] While the use of the actual term "inerrant" has been more recent, it corresponds to the traditional term "infallible." Wesley taught, "'All Scripture is given by inspiration of God'(consequently, all Scripture is infallibly true)."[119]

But it is also anachronistic to claim that Wesley would have adopted the biblical criticism of the nineteenth and twentieth centuries had he been living now. For example, Joel Green states, "To read the Bible as Wesleyans is not to adopt a precritical stance with respect to the nature and interpretation of Scripture." Green goes on to suggest that Wesley would have embraced many developments in biblical criticism.[120] But this is just his assumption. Diane Leclerc wrote that "reading the Bible as a Wesleyan does not imply certain understanding about biblical inspiration and the Bible's authority."[121] Thus, we are given permission to reject Wesley's view of inspiration and authority, while still claiming to be Wesleyan.

In the Fall 2011 issue of the *Wesleyan Theological Journal*, Stephen Gunter declared that inerrancy is *not* the issue for evangelical Wesleyans.[122] Instead he argues for soteriological sufficiency, that the Scripture is sufficient for

---

[118]Wesley, *Journal*, 24 July, 1776.

[119]Wesley, "The Means of Grace," Sermon # 16, 3. 8.

[120]Green, "Is There a Contemporary Wesleyan Hermeneutic?" in *Reading the Bible in Wesleyan Ways*, Barry L. Callen and Richard P. Thompson, eds. (Kansas City: Beacon Hill, 2004), 125.

[121]Leclerc, *Discovering Christian Holiness* (Kansas City: Beacon Hill, 2010), 37. Dr. Leclerc is a professor at Northwest Nazarene University.

[122]Gunter, "Beyond the Bible Wars: Why Inerrancy is not the Issue for Evangelical Wesleyans," *Wesleyan Theological Journal* 46:2 (Fall 2011) 56-69. Dr. Gunter is a professor at Duke Divinity School.

our salvation. Yet many evangelical Wesleyans are unwilling to abandon the doctrine of full inerrancy and are concerned about the direction of Wesleyan theology.

Is Inerrancy Exclusively a Calvinistic Doctrine?

In our evaluation of the doctrine of biblical inerrancy, we must move beyond simply labeling it as a Calvinistic doctrine. To employ the technique of guilt by association is a logical fallacy. Throughout its history the Wesleyan Theological Society has dialogued with process theology and open theism, pentecostal/charismatic theology, postmodernism, Eastern orthodoxy, feminism, and Marxism — just to name a few of their ecumenical dialogues. In every instance they have attempted to objectively discuss areas of compatibility and incompatibility. But they have inconsistently rejected the doctrine of biblical inerrancy by simply labeling it as "Calvinistic." Shouldn't these issues be evaluated on their own merit and not be rejected because of guilt by association? In order to be consistent, must we also reject the doctrines of the Trinity or the virgin birth simply because Calvinists affirm these doctrines?

Wesley himself declared that his theology was but a hairbreadth from Calvinism, and Oden documents that Wesley built on a strong Calvinistic heritage.[123]

Abraham Lincoln once said, "I must stand with anybody that stands right, and stand with him while he is right, and part with him when he goes wrong." A conservative Wesleyan may have more in common with a conservative Calvinist than he does with neo-orthodoxy, process theology, or the higher criticism of liberalism.

---

[123]Wesley, Letter to John Newton, 24 May 1765; Oden, *John Wesley's Teachings* (Grand Rapids: Zondervan, 2012), 148-164. Wesley, however, rejected the Calvinistic doctrine of double predestination.

While it was old Princeton Calvinists like B. B. Warfield and Charles Hodge who developed a more detailed doctrine of inerrancy, they did so in reaction to the liberal attacks on Scripture which were beginning to come from within the church. Prior to this era, attacks upon the integrity of Scripture had come from outside the church. Yet the Calvinist Cornelius Van Til characterized the Princeton "common sense" apologetic as "Arminian" since it was based on evidentialism and rationalism and not presuppositionalism.[124] Thus, Van Til dismissed former Princeton Calvinist faculty members by utilizing this same guilt-by-association technique. Any serious discussion of doctrine must move beyond pejorative labels.

Do Wesleyans Uphold Biblical Fundamentals?

The term "fundamental" refers to basic, rudimentary, foundational, or cardinal principles. Any listing of primary Wesleyan doctrines could be referred to as "fundamental" Wesleyan doctrines.

However, Wesley wrote that in his day the term fundamental was an ambiguous word and that there had been many warm disputes about the number of "fundamentals."[125] Yet he also referred to justification by faith as a "fundamental doctrine of the gospel,"[126] he adds the new birth as another funda-

[124]Van Til, *The Defense of the Faith* (Philadelphia: Presbyterian & Reformed, 1955), 264-265; 279. Van Til also made this accusation directly at Warfield in Van Til, *The Protestant Doctrine of Scripture* (Philadelphia: den Dulk Foundation, 1967), 57.

[125]Wesley, "On the Trinity," Sermon #55, §2.

[126]Wesley, "The Lord Our Righteousness," Sermon #20, § 5.

mental,[127] and Christian perfection and Christlikeness as "the fundamentals of Christianity."[128]

The Fundamentalist Movement began in America after World War I. Originally, this movement defended the inspiration and inerrancy of Scripture, the virgin birth of Christ, his substitutionary atonement, his bodily resurrection, and the historical reality of the miracles of Jesus.

In 1923, J. B. Chapman, then editor of the *Nazarene Herald of Holiness* wrote, "Of course, our sympathies are entirely with the Fundamentalists and we rejoice in their boldness for God and truth. . . . May God bless and prosper all who stand up for God and His Holy Book!"[129]

Later Chapman wrestled with this terminology. He stated that Nazarenes believed in the fundamentals and then proceeded to give his list of fundamental doctrines. However, if the question is raised whether Nazarenes are Fundamentalists, using the term as a proper noun, Chapman answered, "Yes, with reservations." While Chapman had reservations about certain Calvinistic tendencies among Fundamentalists, he had no reservation, however, concerning the inerrancy of Scripture.[130] H. C. Morrison, founder of Asbury Theological Seminary, also maintained a close relationship with the early Fundamentalists.[131]

The thesis of *Square Peg: Why Wesleyans Aren't Fundamentalists* is that denominations in the Wesleyan tradi-

---

[127]Wesley, "The New Birth," Sermon #45, 1-2.

[128]Wesley, "Upon our Lord's Sermon on the Mount, Discourse the Third," Sermon #23, IV. See also Wesley, "On God's Vineyard," Sermon #107, 5.5.

[129]Chapman, "The Victories of the Fundamentalists," *Herald of Holiness* (7 Feb 1923) 2-3.

[130]Chapman, "What is Fundamentalism?" *Herald of Holiness* (6 Oct 1916).

[131]Kenneth Kinghorn, *The Story of Asbury Theological Seminary* (Lexington, KY: Emeth, 2010), 53-62.

tion cannot adopt fundamentalism without forfeiting essential parts of what it means to be Wesleyan. But the real question is whether or not Wesleyans can affirm and defend biblical fundamentals without being dismissed as "Fundamentalists."

The contributors of this book assure us that words like "infallibility" and "inerrancy" do not represent well how we Wesleyans think about Scripture. Yet these modern "Wesleyans" claim it really does not matter if Moses wrote the Pentateuch or whether Isaiah wrote the entire book of Isaiah.[132] Jesus Christ is the real truth of Scripture. Thus Dunning declared that although there may be minor errors in the biblical text, truth is God's saving purpose embodied in Christ.[133]

But if Jesus Christ believed Moses wrote the Pentateuch and that Isaiah wrote Isaiah, then the trustworthiness of Jesus Christ is under question. There are thirteen passages in the Gospels where Jesus upholds the Mosaic authorship of the Pentateuch (for example: Luke 16:31; Mark 10:5; John 5:46). Jesus also quoted from "both parts" of the book of Isaiah and attributed both parts to Isaiah. John 12:39-41and Mark 7:6-7 cited from the first half and Luke 4:17-19 cites from the "second" Isaiah.

John R. W. Stott argued that the reason we submit to the authority of Scripture is that Jesus Christ authenticated it as possessing the authority of God. He endorsed the Old Testament, upholding its divine origin, interpreting his own messianic mission in the light of its prophecies, and taught that certain things *must* come to pass because the Scripture *must* be fulfilled.

---

[132]G. K. Beale, "A Specific Problem Confronting the Authority of the Bible: Should the New Testament's Claim That the Prophet Isaiah Wrote the Whole Book of Isaiah Be Taken at Face Value," *The Erosion of Inerrancy in Evangelicalism* (Wheaton, IL: Crossway, 2008), 123-159.

[133]Dunning, "Comparing and Contrasting: Some Distinguishing Wesleyan and Fundamentalist Expressions of the Christian Faith," *Square Peg*, 66.

Stott then asserted that Jesus Christ made provision for the writing of the New Testament by calling the apostles to record and interpret what he was doing and saying. These apostles were on a par with the Old Testament prophets.

Stott concluded that Christ's view of Scripture must become ours, since the disciple is not above his teacher. "Our doctrine of Scripture is bound up with our loyalty to Jesus Christ. If he is our Teacher and our Lord, we have no liberty to disagree with him. Our view of Scripture must be his."[134]

The term "fundamental" refers to basic, rudimentary, foundational, or cardinal principles. Any listing of primary Wesleyan doctrines could be referred to as "fundamental" Wesleyan doctrines. For example, A. M. Hills, *Fundamental Christian Theology* (1931) or Edwin Mouzon, *Fundamentals of Methodism* (1923) or Donald Haynes, *On the Threshold of Grace: Methodist Fundamentals* (2010).

In their series on "Fundamental Theology," Paulist Press has a title *Fidelity without Fundamentalism* (2010). Therefore it is imperative that we define the term.

Although he did not particularly like the term, J. Gresham Machen defined fundamentalism as "all those who definitely and polemically maintain a belief in supernatural Christianity as over against the Modernism of the present day."[135]

The spirit of *The Fundamentals* (1910-1915) was an ecumenical defense of fundamental Christian orthodoxy. But there is also a narrow, bigoted fundamentalist attitude which

---

[134]Stott, *God's Book for God's People* (Downers Grove, IL: InterVarsity, 1982), 38. See also Stott, *The Authority of the Bible* (Downers Grove, IL: InterVarsity, 1974), 28-29.

[135]Machen, "Does Fundamentalism Obstruct Social Progress? The Negative," *The Survey* 52:7 (1 July 1924) 391.

denounces everyone who does not agree with them on nonessentials. Dunning seems to recognize this ambiguity.[136]

I am not contending that Wesleyans must be Fundamentalists, with a capital F, but we dare not abandon the fundamentals of the faith — call them what you will. There is no need to abandon the inerrancy of Scripture because it is a "fundamentalist" belief.

I am concerned that some, such as Edwin Crawford, are also ready to abandon the label "evangelical" because it is also too Calvinistic.[137] The Greek word *euangelion* means "gospel" and is the basis for our word "evangelical." I hope we are not abandoning the Gospel.

The problem with a "fundamentalist" approach to Scripture is said to be their belief in propositional infallibility. Here again, we must define our terms. A proposition is a statement which is open to either verification or negation. Propositional truth is a statement in which a predicate or object is affirmed or denied regarding a subject. Thus, when Gunter asserts that one cannot be consistently both a Wesleyan and a Fundamentalist, he is making a propositional statement. We all make propositional statements.

Wesleyans do not necessarily reject the validity of propositional truth. The issue of propositional versus existential truth is not either/or but both/and. We are affirming propositional truth every time we recite the Apostles' Creed or affirm our Articles of Religion. Any listing of non-negotiables would be a list of propositions. However, faith must go beyond

---

[136]Dunning, "Comparing and Contrasting: Some Distinguishing Wesleyan and Fundamentalist Expressions of the Christian Faith," *Square Peg*, 63-64.

[137]Leclerc, *Discovering Christian Holiness*, 301. Dr. Crawford was a professor at Northwest Nazarene University for thirty-three years.

As early as 1988 Donald Dayton refused to be called an evangelical [Dayton, "The Holiness Witness in the Ecumenical Church," *Wesleyan Theological Journal* 23:1-2 (Spring-Fall 1988) 98].

propositions. Wesleyans also believe that the Holy Spirit works above and beyond our rational abilities.

The real problem is when our faith is reduced to a set of propositions to be affirmed. It is claimed that propositional truth leads to bibliolatry. According to James 2:19, even the demons affirm the proposition that God exists. Yet the affirmation of that proposition has not saved them. Wesleyan theology believes there must be an existential moment and a transformed life. According to the majority evangelical view of Romans 7, the Holy Spirit can produce a manuscript without error but not an apostle without sin.

Alister McGrath explained that if Christianity "appears to be book-centered it is because it is through the words of Scripture that the believer encounters and feeds upon Jesus Christ."[138] Thus, Wesley could say, "He hath written it down in a book. O give me that book! At any price give me the Book of God!"

According to 1 John 5:10, those who truly believe have the direct testimony or assurance of God through his Spirit. But how do we know that we are not deceived? The epistle of 1 John teaches that if we have the Spirit, we will also affirm the proposition that Jesus is the Christ.

If propositional truth alone may lead to legalism, existential truth alone may lead to antinomianism. Everything is not existential. There must be an absolute point of reference. The biblical teaching is that everything is established by a dual witness. Wesley taught a direct *and* indirect witness. Existential truth must be affirmed by propositional truth. To deny this cuts scripture off from any objective, external verification. Jesus asked, "If I speak to you concerning earthly things, and you do not believe me, how then will you believe if I speak of heavenly things?" (John 3:12).

---

[138]McGrath, *Intellectuals Don't Need God & Other Modern Myths* (Grand Rapids: Zondervan, 1993), 21.

The Scripture, though propositional, is encountered by humans existentially. We come to know it is the Word of God through the *testimonium Spiritus sancti*. John Calvin applied the doctrine of the witness of the Spirit to the internal testimony of the Spirit persuading the regenerate that God is the author of Scripture. The Wesleyan doctrine of the witness of the Spirit is directed toward personal assurance of justification and adoption. But both applications of the doctrine are existential.

However, Mormons also claim that we can know the book of Mormon is from God through a "burning in the bosom." Yet we know that the book of Mormon contains anachronisms and historical inaccuracies. Therefore, our subjective experience must be affirmed through objective verification. If existential realities have no basis in propositional truth, they cannot be valid. There is something about the Word of God, in and of itself, that makes it the Word of God. It does not depend upon our encounter with it to make it the word of God.

On the other hand, the theology of Phoebe Palmer tended to emphasize a propositional syllogism without the direct existential witness. Christian perfection was to be claimed on the basis of a naked or bare faith in certain propositions without any direct existential assurance. Romans 8:16 is a propositional statement promising an existential fulfillment. Thus, we need not reject propositional truth, but we must maintain its balance with existential truth.

J. S. Whale wrote,

> We have to get somehow from *mandata Dei* [the commandments of God] to *Deus mandans* [the commanding God] if our study of Christian doctrine is to mean anything vital. We want a living synthesis where those very facts, which the intellect dissects and coldly examines, are given back to us with the

wholeness which belongs to life. . . . Instead of putting off our shoes from our feet because the place whereon we stand is holy ground, we are taking nice photographs of the burning Bush, from suitable angles: we are chatting about theories of Atonement with our feet on the mantlepiece, instead of kneeling down before the wounds of Christ.[139]

Is there a Wesleyan Hermeneutic?

Dr. Staples once wrote me saying, "I wish you would develop a truly Wesleyan hermeneutic."[140] He recommended that I read Ray Dunning's article "A Wesleyan View of Scripture." However, the article does not demonstrate that Wesley operated from a different hermeneutic than the Protestant historical-grammatical principle.[141]

Canonical criticism accepts the Bible, regardless of whether it is trustworthy, because the Church tells us it is our starting point. Now we are told by a church which affirms at least some of Wesley's doctrine that we should approach the Bible with a Wesleyan hermeneutic.

---

[139]Whale, *Christian Doctrine* (London: Fontana, 1957), 146.

[140]Staples email to Vic Reasoner, 10 January 1998.

[141]Dunning," A Wesleyan View of Scripture," *The Preacher's Magazine* (Dec-Feb 1998) 14-17. See Mark Weeter, "John Wesley vs. John Calvin-Is There A Wesleyan Hermeneutic?" <www.wesleyan.org/bgs/assets/downloads/Doctrinal%20Symposium/2009/down.php?dfile=Weeter paper.pdf>

Weeter advocates a grammatico-historical method and concedes there is not much difference in the hermeneutics of Wesley and Calvin, except that Calvin seems to approach the text with certain assumptions. Why should Wesleyans do the same thing? Our goal should be objectivity, not to advocate starting with Wesleyan assumptions. Calvin was much more objective as a commentator than he was as a theologian.

It has become popular to advocate that Wesleyans use a "Wesleyan hermeneutic."[142] But what is called a "hermeneutic" is actually an a priori presupposition. If I did not start with a Wesleyan hermeneutic would I arrive at Wesleyan conclusions?

Joel B. Green introduced his book, *Reading Scripture as Wesleyans*, by asking, "How do we know if the Bible is 'true,' then? If it shows us the way to heaven." While he defines the way to heaven as the journey of salvation, there are many proposed ways of salvation. Green however avoids this crucial question by writing,

> There are other ways to read the Bible, to be sure. But Methodists locate their reading of the Bible within the larger Wesleyan tradition. We read the Bible as Wesleyans. And we need to know what this looks like.

Green advocates a process of observation in which we see how Wesley held certain assumptions about the nature of Scripture. But if I observe that Wesley held the Scriptures to be fully inspired, fully inerrant, and therefore our final authority, Green would react that being Wesleyan is "not in the sense of marching lockstep to his cadence or matching his gait with our own."[143]

In her recent book *Discovering Christian Holiness*, Diane Leclerc affirms that the Bible stands above the three handmaids of tradition, reason, and experience. However, chapter one, "How to read the Bible as a Wesleyan," implies that we approach the Bible with a certain philosophic presupposition.

---

[142]See *Reading the Bible in Wesleyan Ways: Some Constructive Proposals*, Barry L. Callen and Richard P. Thompson, eds. (Kansas City: Beacon Hill, 2004).

[143]Joel B. Green, *Reading Scripture as Wesleyans* (Nashville: Abingdon, 2010), ix-x.

This, however, may result in an interpretation which differs from Wesley himself.

Wesley, of course, is not our final authority. He explained in "The Character of a Methodist" (1742),

> We believe, indeed, that "all Scripture is given by the inspiration of God;" and herein we are distinguished from Jews, Turks, and infidels. We believe the written word of God to be the *only and the sufficient* rule both of Christian faith and practice; and herein we are fundamentally distinguished from those of the Romish Church. We believe Christ to be the Eternal, Supreme God; and herein we are distinguished from the Socinians and Arians. But as to all opinions which do not strike at the root of Christianity, we "think and let think." So that whatsoever they are, whether right or wrong, they are no "distinguishing marks" of a Methodist.[144]

Here Wesley distinguishes between fundamental Christian doctrines and secondary opinions. We may disagree with Wesley on secondary issues and still be within the Wesleyan tradition. However, it is not Wesleyan to undercut the authority of Scripture.

There was nothing unique to Wesley about his hermeneutic. He utilized Reformation hermeneutics — the grammatical-historical approach. Leclerc describes Wesley's approach as inductive, yet she states her conclusions *before* ever approaching scripture. Basically, we are to accept Wesley's order of salvation and so when we read the Bible we read those presuppositions into the text. Yet Calvinists read the same scripture with their own presuppositions and arrive at very different conclusions. There can be no objective proof whether either

---

[144]Wesley, *BE Works*, 9:33-34.

approach is right because we have already stripped the Bible of its final authority.

Yet she is critical of Wesley's views on biblical authority and is sure that we should reject biblical inerrancy. We are assured that Wesley would have adopted the biblical criticism of the nineteenth and twentieth centuries had he been living now. Therefore, we are given permission to reject Wesley's view of inspiration and authority, but we must read the Bible with Wesley's analogy of faith — yet realizing he may not be right![145]

We would be better served to reject this subjective, so-called "Wesleyan hermeneutic" and instead return to Wesley's objective view of Scripture. The real battle is whether we should utilize a grammatical-historical hermeneutic or a critical-historical hermeneutic which utilizes destructive higher criticism. This "hermeneutic first" approach is analogous to modern schools of journalism which stress advocacy rather than objectivity. If God's Word is forever settled in heaven (Psalm 119:89), it serves no useful purpose to undermine its full authority here on earth.

CONCLUSION

Writing in 2011 the Board of General Superintendents of the Wesleyan Church said,

> Wesleyans, however, hold steadfastly and unapologetically to the Holy Scriptures of the Old and New Testaments as God's inspired, infallible, inerrant, and supremely authoritative guide for Christian faith and conduct. We regard God's revealed truth as absolute (that is, it is valid in all

---

[145]*Discovering Christian Holiness: The Heart of Wesleyan-Holiness Theology* (Kansas City: Beacon Hill, 2010), 33-49. Ironically, the foreword is written by Rob L. Staples.

> times and places); the canonical revelation as complete (in other words, not open to addition by "new revelations" or subtraction by modern revisionist interpreters); and historic Christian faith and practice as wiser counsel than opinion polls or majority votes (although tradition is not in and of itself authoritative and is always subject to correction by the Word of God).[146]

However, contemporary theologians within the Wesleyan tradition have claimed that this position is not truly Wesleyan.

The Protestant Reformation declared Scripture alone to be our final authority. Martin Luther said, "A layman who has Scripture is more than Pope or council without it." Another time Luther objected,

> I asked for Scriptures and you offer me the Fathers. I ask for the sun and he shows me his lanterns. I ask "Where is your Scripture proof" and he cited the Fathers. With all due respect to the Fathers I prefer the authority of the Scriptures.

When he was asked to recant before the Diet of Worms he replied,

> Unless I am convinced by the testimony of the Scriptures or by clear reason, I am bound by the Scriptures I have quoted, and my conscience is captive to the Word of God. I cannot and I will not retract anything, since it is neither safe nor right to go against conscience. Here I stand, I can do nothing else.

---

[146]"Pastoral Letter on Homosexuality," *Board of General Superintendents of the Wesleyan Church* (May 2011) 6.

These modern attacks upon the authority of God's Word take the Bible from the hands of the common man. Who decides which parts of Scripture are trustworthy?

The doctrine of complete inerrancy is vital because the *sola scriptura* principle, that Scripture is our final authority, cannot be maintained without it. Anyone who declares there are mistakes in the Scripture is setting himself or herself up as an authority above Scripture.

For Further Reading

This short booklet was never intended to be the final word. My purpose was to introduce a defense of biblical inerrancy to contemporary Wesleyans. It began as an article submitted to the *Wesleyan Theological Journal* which was rejected in March 2012.

The International Council on Biblical Inerrancy functioned from 1978-1986. During that time they produced at least eight books, all of which are helpful.

Boice, James Montgomery, ed. *The Foundation of Biblical Authority*. Grand Rapids: Zondervan, 1978. Chapters by seven leading evangelicals.

Carson, D. A. and John D. Woodbridge, eds. *Scripture and Truth*. 2nd ed. Grand Rapids: Baker, 1992. Twelve chapters by leading evangelicals deal with biblical, historical, and theological questions.

Geisler, Norman L, ed. *Inerrancy*. Grand Rapids: Zondervan, 1980. Chapters by fourteen leading evangelical scholars based on papers they presented at the original ICBI in 1978.

_______, ed. *Biblical Errancy: An Analysis of its Philosophical Roots*. Grand Rapids: Zondervan, 1981. Eight chapters by leading evangelicals.

Hannah, John D. ed. *Inerrancy and the Church.* Chicago: Moody, 1984. Wilber T. Dayton's chapter, "Infallibility, Wesley, and British Wesleyanism" and Daryl E. McCarthy's chapter, "Inerrancy in American Wesleyanism" are worth the price of this book.

Kantzer, Kenneth S. ed., *Applying The Scriptures.* Grand Rapids: Zondervan, 1987. Seventeen chapters and responses from ICBI Summit III dealing with the practical consequences of the doctrine of inerrancy.

Lewis, Gordon R. And Bruce Demarest, eds. *Challenges to Inerrancy: A Theological Response.* Chicago: Moody, 1984. Chapters by thirteen evangelical theologians.

Radmacher, Earl and Robert Preus, eds. *Hermeneutics, Inerrancy, and the Bible.* Grand Rapids: Zondervan, 1984. Chapters by sixteen evangelical scholars from ICBI Summit II dealing with biblical interpretation. Each chapter is followed by two responses.

Historically, evangelicals have always defended the authority of Scripture. That is why it is disconcerting to have modern evangelical "Wesleyans" doing the work of the skeptics.

Archer, Gleason L. *Encyclopedia of Biblical Difficulties.* Grand Rapids: Zondervan, 1982.

Kaiser, Walter C, Peter H. Davids, F. F. Bruce, Manfred T. Brauch. *Hard Sayings of the Bible*. Downers Grove, IL: InterVarsity, 1996.

After the ICBI disbanded as planned, the liberals never went to bed. Thus there has been a need to articulate the doctrine of an inerrant Scripture to a new generation. Here are some recent attempts:

Beale, G. K. *The Erosion of Inerrancy in Evangelicalism.* Wheaton, IL: Crossway, 2008. The first four chapters are a response to Peter Enns who was suspended from the faculty of Westminster Theological Seminary in 2008. The rest of the book offers solutions to Old Testament problem passages, especially where they appear to conflict with modern science.

Geisler, Norman L. and William C. Roach. *Defending Inerrancy.* Grand Rapids: Baker, 2011.

Hoffmeier, James K. and Dennis R. Magary, eds. *Do Historical Matters Matter to Faith?* Wheaton, IL: Crossway, 2012.

Merrick, James R. A. *Five Views on Biblical Inerrancy.* Grand Rapids: Zondervan, 2013.

Endorsements for The Importance of Inerrancy

Dr. Reasoner has brought another set of lucid insights to the arena where the "Battle for the Bible" continues to rage. May I say with Harold Lindsell, the one-time editor of *Christianity Today*, it is still the watershed issue. Where you fall on this "continental divide" determines where you and your influence will "flow" to its legacy. It is interesting that *The Wesleyan Theological Journal* which recently published a contrary view, elected not to vet, in follow-up, the historical, orthodox view of Scripture, and that of historical Wesleyanism, nonetheless.

However, Dr. Reasoner's rebuttal is powerful. The book you hold in your hands is an expansion of the substance set forth in that rejected article. Many of us concur with Dr. Reasoner, "all scripture is God-breathed and (all) are profitable." We contest the implications of the inerrancy antagonists who believe that not all scripture, just some, has soteriological inerrancy. These are *almost* not antagonists at all, who believe that God inerrantly revealed the *way of salvation*, but are unwilling to battle for the inerrancy of Scripture when it comes to its statements regarding science, history, cultural and social matters. It all matters! They who have missed the mark.

These are they who prefer the English Revised Version (1881), "every scripture inspired of God is also profitable," leaving the inference that those that are not inspired are not profitable. However, context, perhaps even syntax, and most assuredly the history of orthodox interpretation concur correctly with "all Scripture is inspired and (all) is profitable."

God is there, has spoken and is true and cannot err. The end of the argument is that God is true and He speaks; therefore, what He has said must be true. The sum of Scripture is the total of its parts. *All are or none is*. The original manuscripts must be true and we have faithful copies.

It is my belief that Dr. Reasoner has produced a helpful, thoughtful response to a trend within Wesleyan-Arminian circles, a trend to give up the fight for total inerrancy. This trend constitutes nothing less than an attack on the "faith that was once and for all delivered to the saints." Jesus defended the total trustworthiness of Scripture and let us be loyal to Him!

"Hammer away, ye hostile hands. Your hammer breaks; God's anvil stands!"
— motto on the seal of a Waldensen church

Dr. Eddie Beaver, Executive Director
The Cornerstone Foundation

* * *

When truth is attacked, God's people need to not only defend it, but forcefully and effectively proclaim it. Dr. Vic Reasoner's booklet does both in a clear and scholarly manner that is easily understood. Biblical inerrancy and infallibility are essential components of the inspiration of Scripture taught in the Bible and are clearly set forth by Dr. Reasoner. I highly recommend it to both pastors and laity.

Rev. Gary K. Briden, Executive Director,
Association of Independent Methodists
Former President, Southern Methodist College

* * *

Dr. Reasoner has done a great service to the Wesleyan community and to the wider body of Christ. He has not only defended the historic orthodox view on the infallibility and inerrancy of Scripture, but he has narrated and documented the erosion of inerrancy among some contemporary evangelicals. I pray that not only Wesleyans but that all other groups will learn from his analysis and reverse course on the current slide from the inerrancy of Scripture. For most current attempts to "redefine" inerrancy are in fact undermining it. The bold truth is that God cannot err, and the Bible is the Word of God. Therefore, the Bible cannot err. Further, the God who cannot err is omniscient (all-knowing), and an omniscient Mind cannot err on any topic it addresses. Thus, as the framers of the ICBI (international Council on Biblical Inerrancy) statement affirmed, the Bible cannot on any area on which it speaks, whether it soteriological (salvation), ethical, historical, or scientific. For those who deviate from this norm, the words of the apostle are appropriate: "Let God be true and every man a liar."

Dr. Norman L. Geisler,
Co-founder of ICBI and Chancellor of
Veritas Evangelical Seminary

* * *

I commend Dr. Vic Reasoner on this work which defines and defends the inspiration and the inerrancy of Scripture. He rightly makes the point that the Bible itself establishes a proper doctrine of inspiration which includes inerrancy of the original manuscripts, and that John Wesley, founder of the Wesleyan-Arminian, Methodist movement, held strongly to the position. Dr. Reasoner sadly shows the academic gymnastics of many who deny total inspiration and inerrancy of the Bible while trying to represent themselves to the church as believing in the inspiration of the Bible. To reduce or minimize the authority of Scripture is to reduce God's authority in some degree, and we must not do that! Thank you "Dr. Vic" for this helpful work which confirms that it is right and academic to believe in the inspiration and inerrancy of the Scriptures.

Dr. John T. Hucks, Jr.
President, The Southern Methodist Church

* * *

While much of Wesleyan theology has drifted so far from the truth of what Wesley himself believed and taught, it is good to have a bastion of truth concerning the topic of Biblical inerrancy such as is found in Dr. Vic Reasoner's, *The Importance of Inerrancy*. As the Christian Education Director of The Southern Methodist Church, and as Director of Light of Life Ministry, Nashville, TN, I am proud to be numbered with those who still believe the Bible to be the inspired, inerrant, infallible, and totally authoritative Word of the Living God. I pray that this important apologetic of inerrancy will get into the hands of all who consider themselves to be 'Wesleyan,' and that the Holy Spirit himself will reveal to them the importance of believing in this foundational truth concerning God's Holy Word. Thank you, Dr. Reasoner, for the academic excellence in this presentation, and for your uncompromised position on this vital topic.

Rev. James O. Jones,
Director, Light of Life Ministry
Director of Christian Education, Southern Methodist Church

* * *

After three years in a relatively liberal evangelical seminary, I graduated in 1986 with a Master of Divinity degree and a lot of questions about the authority of Scripture. My questions came from an honest and authentic search for the truth. I had been reared in a movement that taught plenary inspiration. But three years of claims that Scripture is a very human record of human experiences of God, but not an inerrant word, had eroded my confidence in the Bible.

Since that time, I have taken time to think long and deeply about questions of inerrancy and authority of Scripture. Could Scripture be only partly accurate and remain trustworthy? ***If*** the original autographs contained errors, how can we know which parts are accurate, and which are not? Shall the uninspired presume to judge the words of men into whom God breathed his own Word? How ludicrous.

To be what it claims to be, Scripture must, first and foremost, be true. To be true ***at*** all, Scripture must be true ***in*** all. If Scripture is not accurate in all its parts, we cannot know with certainty which parts are accurate, and which parts are not — not even with centuries of study. If part of Scripture cannot be trusted fully, none of it can be trusted with certainty.

Furthermore, if Scripture is not *completely* trustworthy, it cannot be what it claims to be - authoritative for doctrine, reproof, correction, and instruction in righteousness. An error-pitted Scripture could be no more authoritative than a Zane Grey novel or a Shakespearian tragedy. Scripture ***must be*** inspired, inerrant, and fully trustworthy in order to have any ultimate religious or eternal authority of any kind.

In the booklet you now hold, Dr. Reasoner presents a worthy primer on the importance of this doctrine for the church in general and for those of Wesleyan-Arminian persuasion in particular. If after reading it you still have questions, you will be well on your way toward solid answers for your faith. I am proud to have Dr. Reasoner as a friend and colleague in the International Fellowship of Bible Churches, Inc.

He has summarized our position on the importance of inerrancy very well. I commend this work to you, and pray that God will guide your search for truth.

Dr. William Sillings
General Superintendent
International Fellowship of Bible Churches, Inc.